Lady Wisdom BUILDS A HOUSE!

Building and Leading Well by Establishing Habits of Wisdom

Vol 3: Lady Wisdom Speaks™ Series

DR. CATHERINE CONSTANT

WESTBOW
PRESS®
A DIVISION OF THOMAS NELSON
& ZONDERVAN

WestBow Press books may be ordered through booksellers or by contacting:

WestBow Press
A Division of Thomas Nelson & Zondervan
1663 Liberty Drive
Bloomington, IN 47403
www.westbowpress.com
1 (866) 928-1240

ISBN: 978-1-9736-8961-4 (sc)
ISBN: 978-1-9736-8963-8 (hc)
ISBN: 978-1-9736-8962-1 (e)

Library of Congress Control Number: 2020906419

Print information available on the last page.

WestBow Press rev. date: 4/8/2020

Building and Leading Well by Establishing Habits of Wisdom:

To: _____

From: _____

Date: _____

Contents

Digging the Reservoir of Peace

Establishing the Supply of Goodness

Planning and Developing Kingdom Building

Refining with the Tool of Prayer

Strengthening with the Tool of Praise

Intensifying with the Tool of Thanksgiving

Deepening with the Tool of Worship

Acknowledgments

I dedicate *Lady Wisdom Builds a House!* to my Wisdom Connection Internet Family (Facebook, Instagram, and YouTube) who inspire me to create and share my thoughts and writings. This book is also in recognition of my assignment to help believers, specifically women, draw closer to the Lord and live with courage, strength, and faith, knowing the Lord has blessings and purpose for them. In my book, I desire to encourage my readers to study the book of Proverbs and engage in self-reflection, leading to new perspectives in obtaining the life they desire and deserve.

To my family, Errol, Karen, and Stephen, I am grateful for your support and encouragement that you show me. I love you!

Most of all, I acknowledge my giver of wisdom, insight, and understanding, my heavenly Father. With great sincerity, I am thankful to God for giving me the capacity to write and share His heart concerning His desire for each one of us. I am grateful to Jesus Christ, my Lord and Savior who provided the way for me to grow. I am also thankful for the guidance of Holy Spirit in leading and guiding me in this process of writing this devotional/journal, *Lady Wisdom Builds a House!*

Introduction

I am a blessed, wise, healthy, wealthy woman of integrity and prudence walking in serenity with dignity into my destiny with Jesus Christ. By utilizing my creative, inner genius, I am a builder of family, community, and business, establishing enterprises for now and generations to come.

- "Wisdom has built her house" (Proverbs 9:1 KJV).
- "Wise people are builders—they build families, businesses, communities. And through intelligence and insight their enterprises are established and endure" (Proverbs 24:3 TPT).
- "Any enterprise is built by wise planning, becomes strong through common sense, and profits wonderfully by keeping abreast of the facts" Proverbs 24:3–4 (TLB).
- "For the Lord your God is bringing you into a good land of brooks, pools, gushing springs, valleys and hills, it is a land of wheat and barley, of grapes vines, fig trees, pomegranates, olives, and honey; it is a land where food is plentiful and nothing is lacking; it is a land where iron is as common as stone and copper is abundant in the hills. When you have eaten your fill, bless the Lord your God for the good land he has given you" (Deuteronomy 8:7–10 TLB).

Lady Wisdom tells us that wise planning builds any enterprise. The structure becomes strong through common sense and will be successful. It will be established and profit for generations to come if the leader keeps abreast of the facts. Building houses of applied knowledge and wisdom that meet the needs of our society today will stand the test of time. Allowing our Creator God to provide the blueprint for our destiny through wisdom lifestyle strategies will unfold creative concepts and innovation that will transform our world for God's glory.

Why Did God Create You?

You are a gift to the world—created to worship. Like Jesus, each person is a gift. Father God intended that we bless the world with our lives. God is a God of intentionality and reasoning. He purposely placed each of us on this earth to fulfill His will and plan. We all have something special to offer the world. There is something uniquely assigned for each of us to be and to do. You are an exclusive gift designed for greatness.

Our lives are our gift back to God. It is present in the form of our worship. When we come into God's presence, let our immediate response be to worship Him. We must tell others of who He is and what He has done. Let us react like the shepherds of Christmas and go back glorifying and praising God. Also, like the Magi, we can bow down and worship Jesus by opening our treasure chests and giving Him the gift of our worship.

The Bible, which is Jesus's story, is a road map revealing His purpose and calling. We too have a destiny and a book written about us in heaven. Napoleon Hill called them *envelops*. God gave us a choice to decide our destiny. We are in full control to determine our destiny. Our mind is the most powerful tool we will ever work with. We must take control of our mind to see and connect the consequences with actions.

Thank God for a sound mind. The Holy Spirit is within you to give direction. Direct your mind and create your heaven with your gift of vision and voice. Visions are given to people who capture them and believe that what they perceive is possible. Your voice has been given to you to speak your world into existence and to speak forth your vision. Your words carry authority and power. Speak what God says about your destiny and you. Pray, meditate on God's Word and promises to you, and allow Jesus's favor, wisdom, and power to multiply and grow your dream into something beautiful.

Are you an entrepreneur? Do you want to create something new or expand an innovative idea? An entrepreneur takes on a business idea and is willing to risk failure to accomplish a purpose or dream. The beginning may be small and appear insignificant, but with the appropriate assessment, the idea can grow into something very profitable. Acknowledging a God-ordained idea, assignment, or business venture can lead to great increase, financial wealth, and prosperous relationships.

The dream may appear insignificant and impossible. However, this is not the time to despise the small beginnings but to realize that we have to develop the fruit of patience. Let patience have its perfect work in us. It will take time for things to build. We have to give the seed (time, talent, and treasure) time to germinate. But by biblical meditation, prayer, and worship, we will see changes happen. It may start off little by little, but eventually it will grow into something grand if we stick with it. Have patience!

Lady Wisdom speaks and encourages us to pursue our dreams. She gives us an example of what it looks like to be a wise woman of destiny. "She goes out to inspect a field, and buys it: with her own hands, she plants a vineyard" (Proverbs 31:16 TLB). The Proverbs 31 woman is prudent in her assessment of the risks because she first inspects the field, studying the possibilities and learning the pros and cons of her investment. She is an example of wisdom in action. She is willing to give it scrutiny before purchasing the business, actually counting the cost. I think she was asking herself, "How can I make this field produce a great harvest?"

So it is in the garden ... so it is in your life. Whatever idea, goal, or project you begin starts out as a "small beginning," a seed. As a gardener, I am aware of small beginnings because of the seed. A seed is capable of developing into a plant. So we sow the land with seeds to produce more of what we want to grow. When you look at a seed, it does not seem significant. What can come from this seed?

Yet people who are selling the seed planted it before. They have provided for us a vision of what it can be. By showing a picture on the package, we can determine what the seed has the potential to become. Now each seed produces of its own kind. That is, if you are planting a tomato seed, then you will have tomatoes. If you are planting a lemon seed, then you will have a lemon tree. Both are a seed, yet both have a unique assignment or future. You are a seed in the hand of the Lord!

God has given each of us a seed, or an idea, to build. He provides the investment in you. Don't despise your small beginnings! Have you heard the saying, "Don't eat your seed"? Seed is your time, talent, and treasure. Consider the following:

1. The seed you have received has the potential to be used as food to eat now or to plant for a greater harvest. If you devour your seed (time, talent, or treasure) and do not invest in it, then you would have nothing to put into your business or project.
2. Make sure that wherever you place your seed (time, talent, or treasure), it is "good ground." You can see a return for the effort and work placed in the business or organization. A good seed in bad ground will never produce a harvest.

What does this mean for you? You are God's instrument of change! People around you may despise your dream. The seeds you have may not look significant. God gave you those seeds, and He does not look down on your faith to plant them. So do not despise the little things that you have right now in the form of a seed. See them as your own small garden that holds your blessings. Plant your seed!

You are God's anointed ones. Disregard what people say and place your seeds in the ground before Jesus. Jesus has the power to grow your seeds and multiply your harvest. You are God's builder. Whatever you are building right now in your career, home, business, schooling, or even little garden, don't despise the day of small, little, humble beginnings. Plant your seed!

What Is a Proverb?

The book of Proverbs includes some of the Bible's wisdom literature. A proverb is a type of Hebrew poetry that contains a massive amount of wisdom. A proverb is called a Hebrew *masal*, a poetic, terse, vivid, thought-provoking saying that says a word of truth in a few words. It includes two lines that do not rhyme words but rhythmic concepts. Proverbs are neither commands nor promises.

Proverbs sometimes need to be gathered together with other proverbs on the same subject to obtain the full understanding of the word or complete picture. Many of the proverbs are observations of how to navigate life and what does and does not work in situations. These poetic words carry life lessons and the understanding of the complexities of life.

Studying proverbs requires that one reflects on what is said. It takes time and some effort. That is why Lady Wisdom calls the words "nuggets of truth." Wisdom is something that must be discovered, like gold. The wisdom nuggets, like hard candy, must be savored to get the full flavor and sweetness of the meaning and insight.

Wisdom Habits to Develop

Guided biblical meditation is the process of deliberately focusing on specific thoughts (such as a passage from the book of Proverbs) and reflecting on their meaning in the context of the love of God. Wisdom meditation aims to heighten the understanding of wisdom principles, personal relationships with God, and commitment to developing community. Developing habits of biblical meditation, prayer, and gratitude will empower us to move with confidence and authority in our destiny and transformational ability to win in this life.

Meditating the Word

Psalm 119:11 (KJV) states, "Thy word have I hid in my heart so that I may not sin against thee." Also Psalm 1:2 (KJV) reads, "But his delight is in the law of the LORD and in his law doth he meditates day and night." To meditate the Bible, the Word of God, Robert J. Morgan gives some great strategies for biblical meditation. In his book *Biblical Meditation*, he provides a plan based on biblical meditation: pondering, personalizing, and practicing God's Word. In a quiet place away from distractions and interruptions, he encourages us to follow these strategies.

While meditating on the words of Lady Wisdom, I found the need to add two additional strategies, or "Ps," to the meditation: prayer and praise. We pray to God and ask Him to guide us through the scriptures. Next, we read and ponder the Word. Then we personalize the meaning as we interpret what the Word is saying to us. Now we practice the Word and determine how we will fulfill it in our daily life. Finally we praise God for activating His Word in our spirit and minds. We now have the five Ps: pray, ponder, personalize, practice, and praise.

Pray

God's will for our lives through His Word is revealed when we pray. We must pray and ask Him to show Himself to us. We want the Holy Spirit to illuminate the Word before us. We desire a spirit-to-spirit connection. 1 Corinthians 2:16 tells us that we have the mind of Christ and know the plan, purpose, and perspective of Christ. James 1:5 states that if we lack wisdom, we can ask God and He will give it to us. Therefore, we can know God's plan for our lives.

Ponder

Pondering requires that we read the passage of scripture aloud. Imagine the Lord is talking to you in a personal way. Focus on each word and pay attention to the meaning. You must have a desire to understand what the passage is saying.

Personalize

Think about what the scripture means to you. Read it thoughtfully, considering, "What does this say to me for my body, mind, soul, and spirit?" Think of this as a personal reflection, letting the Holy Spirit speak to your heart. If the Holy Spirit were sitting next to you, what verse, phrase, word, truth command, or promise would affect you the most?

Practice

Write down that verse, phrase, word, truth, command, or promise and think about it throughout the day. When you have quiet times during the day, think about the word you are meditating on. Think about it all day when you shower, drive the car, walk up steps, work at the desk, or daydream in a chair. Most of all, think about it when you are going to sleep. You can also share it with a friend or someone who may need a right word for the day. You can share it on your social media platforms like Facebook. Finally put it into practice by being obedient to what the Word of God says for you to do. Practice it.

Praise

When we do God's will, we must do it with joy. The joy of the Lord will strengthen us to follow through with what the Lord has commanded us to do. It would not become a chore or a burden. Instead of praise and thanksgiving, we can walk out our promises with the expectation that God will answer our prayers and help us to become more like Him.

As you read through the devotional readings, follow these suggestions:

- **Ponder:** Read the passage of scripture aloud. Imagine the Lord is talking to you in a personal way. Focus on each word and pay attention to the meaning.
- **Personalize:** Think about what the scripture means to you. Read it thoughtfully, considering, "What is this saying to me concerning my body, mind, soul, and spirit?"
- **Practice:** Write down the verse, phrase, word, truth command, or promise and think about it throughout the day and when you go to sleep. Look for opportunities to apply the word.
- **Pray:** Ask God what He wants to reveal to you in this verse. Tell Him that you want a spirit-to-spirit connection so you can know Christ's plan, purpose, and perspective.
- **Praise:** Let joy rise in your heart and thank God for sharing His wisdom with you. You can sing, shout, dance, write, and declare God's goodness to you.

Write the Vision

Writing your thoughts in the devotional/journal is highly recommended. It is essential to journal what the Lord has revealed to you. As you write down the words, it then becomes a part of your thought process. You can retrieve the word and regain possession of the promise. This process will enable you to follow the plan with more accuracy and help you to bring fidelity to the series of steps for you to reach a positive result.

Speak the Vision

Your voice has been given to you to speak your world into existence and to speak forth your vision. Your words carry authority and power. It is time to declare with your words, the vision and voice what you see into existence. We must ask God to transform our vision to what He sees and to give us the words to say so we will speak what He does.

Speaking what God says about you and your destiny releases a wise strategy needed to establish enterprises that will endure. The release of the revelation-knowledge increases strength to complete the assignment. Courage to keep on building is realized, especially when the manifestation of what has been said is revealed.

My prayer for you is that you will learn how to apply wisdom, knowledge, and understanding to your life as you build Jesus's kingdom. I hope that you will boldly rely on God's faithfulness to mature you into the blessed, wise, healthy, wealthy person that Lady Wisdom intends for you to be.

Thank you for constructing with me *Lady Wisdom Builds a House!* as we explore the process of living and loving well. You are discovering you!

Joyfully in Christ,
Dr. Catherine Constant

Building the Foundation of

LOVE

1

Love: Blessing of Energy

How does a man become wise? The first step
is to trust and reverence the Lord!
—Proverbs1:7 (TLB)

Lady Wisdom asks, "Have you checked your energy source?"

Energy is generated from the force of love. When we love someone or something, we can stir up the power to demonstrate the passion for it. We become excited with the opportunity to express our affections to the person. The zeal is there and then becomes translated into energy. So it is with whatever we genuinely love. Jesus answered him, "Love the Lord your God with every passion of your heart, with all the energy of your being and with every thought that is within you" (Matthew 22:37 TPT).

As a gardener, I have discovered that the energy to love my garden starts with passion from my heart. Our emotions lead us to do things. Enthusiasm for the garden can help us see the garden with brand-new eyes. We know what it can become. The possibilities are there, and we want to bring them to fruition. Our actions demonstrate the energy for the garden. We plan the garden, prepare the soil, buy the seeds, plant the seeds, cultivate the land, and then reap the harvest.

We can create energy in our gardens that is both positive and therapeutic for the mind, body, soul, and spirit. Spending time there gives us the ability to improve our health, reduce stress, and increase our clarity about life and any issues. The garden blesses us with positive energy, which gives us a sense of well-being.

Plant a tree. Trees improve the quality of the air and give us more oxygen to breathe. Trees absorb sound, buffer noise pollution, and provide shelter for wildlife. Add a bench or sitting area or create an indoor space to view your garden. There you will gain energy by soaking up the sounds and sights of the garden, which will generate love in your heart and increase the strength to work.

Prayer
Dear Lord, Please increase energy of love and a passion to do Your will. By Your love, I want a peaceful environment to be established in my life. I want to generate a willingness to be proactive and not reactive. I also desire to work diligently in the garden of my heart with the energy of love to obtain the serenity I desire. Thank you. Amen.

Word of the Day
Energy

Personal Meditations

Today's Prayer

2

Love: Agape Love

He wrote them to teach his people how to live-how to
act in every circumstance, for he wanted them to be
understanding, just and fair in everything they did.
—Proverbs 1:2 (TLB)

Lady Wisdom asks, "How are you demonstrating your love?"

There is a great reward with agape love, one that is redeeming and transforming. A characteristic of the love described in Proverbs is the demonstration of love. It is what we do for others. In the month of February, we celebrate Valentine's Day. We recognize the one whom we have romantic attractions for, and they recognize us. We may receive a box of chocolates, a card, or maybe some jewelry. The person will say "I love you." This expression of love makes us feel good inside and excited about being appreciated and acknowledged by the person whom we have the same feelings for. But is there more to love than that?

I believe that there is. There are many layers to love. There is the surface love. For example, "I love that dress" or "I love my car." We see the value or emotional appreciation for things. There is a desire to obtain things that give us enjoyment and/or pleasure. So our response is, "I love that!" There is also a love that is directed at self. Most people's concept of love is self-centered, a love that demands something in return.

But there is a higher form of love, agape love. Agape love is unconditional, divine love, which Jesus Christ modeled. "For God so loved the world that He gave his only begotten Son" (John 3:16 KJV). This kind of love transcends our human understanding and requires that we look outside of ourselves and love others.

We have to explore what true love is. Can we find answers in the book of Proverbs concerning this important need and human experience? I know we can, and we are going to ask Lady Wisdom to show us the way to a deeper experience in the understanding of love. In Proverbs 1:2, King Solomon loves his people and wants to see them be successful in life. He performs an unselfish act by asking God for wisdom to be able to lead his people in the ways of wisdom. King Solomon was ready to give agape love, despite the sacrifice involved. It is the reasoning, esteeming, and making-wise-decisions type of love that benefits all.

Prayer
Dear Lord, Help me to discover agape love. There is a great reward with agape love, a love that is redeeming and transforming. Amen.

Word of the Day
Demonstrating

Personal Meditations

Today's Prayer

3

Love: Trust and Revere the Lord

How does a man [woman] become wise? The first
step is to trust and reverence the Lord!
—Proverbs 1:7 (TLB)

Lady Wisdom asks, "How do you demonstrate love for the Lord?"

The highest form of love is when we trust and respect someone. We are
recognizing their presence. Acknowledging the existence, validity, and
greatness of God places us in a position to know Him to the fullest. In
the book of Hebrews, it says we must believe that God is and that He
rewards those who diligently seek Him.

To take this experience even further, we also have to develop trust for
God. It is difficult to trust someone if we do not have a relationship with
them. God wants to have a relationship with us. That is why He sent
his Son Jesus as a representative of His love and grace. That is, while
we were still sinners committing immoral acts and going against His
divine law, Christ Jesus died for us so we could know Father God. It is
unconditional love, divine love—*agape* love.

At the heart of agape love is sacrifice, and I believe that is why it becomes
difficult for many to pursue God because it requires that we humble
ourselves and follow Him. We have to sacrifice our ways of doing things
to follow His way. However, if we realize that God loves us, we can
then release our fears and doubts. We can walk in confidence and faith
knowing that God has our best interest at heart. He loves us!

Prayer

Dear Lord, I know You have great plans for us to prosper and to give us a great future. Please make us willing to take the first step in the process of love and humble ourselves. Help us to let Your will be done in our lives so we will trust and revere Your *agape* love. Amen.

Word of the Day
Respect

Personal Meditations

Today's Prayer

4

Love: Love Speaks!

Come here and listen to me! I'll pour out the spirit
of wisdom upon you and make you wise.
—Proverbs 1:23 (TLB)

Lady Wisdom asks, "What does the voice of love sound like to you?"

Lady Wisdom speaks and says she is calling, "I have called you so often
but still you won't come. I have pleaded, but all in vain. For you have
spurned my counsel and reproof. Someday you'll be in trouble, and I'll
laugh! Mock me, will you?—I'll mock you!" (Proverbs 1:24–26 TLB).

We have a responsibility to act on the love that is given to us. We must
receive! In order to be transformed inside and to reflect beauty outside
to the world, we have to decide to come and listen. Wisdom will provide
the anointing, the pouring out of the spirit of wisdom, to clean us up
so we can shine.

When our love increases with more knowledge and discernment, then
we become strengthened in our inner human, where Christ dwells. We
are rooted and grounded in love and can understand what love is all
about. We start to glimpse Christ's love, which passes knowledge, and
all the fullness of God and His love (Ephesians 3:16–19) fill us. When
the radiance of His love shines through us to others, we are beautiful!

We are going to need God's love and the spirit of wisdom to be able
to interact with others so our voice has the sound of love. It is difficult
to love people who test your ability to love. Even Lady Wisdom had
to experience this too, but she is still calling. Yes, she is still speaking!

Even though people may treat you badly, you must find a way to allow the fruit of the spirit and the spirit of wisdom to override those negative thoughts and go forward with love. Pray for them, bless them, and do good things for them because you want to be obedient to the voice of love.

Prayer
Dear Lord, I have a responsibility to act on the love that is given to me. I must receive it to become transformed inside and to be able to reflect the beauty outside to the world. Help me to humble myself and listen to Your instructions. Amen.

Word of the Day
Voice

Personal Meditations

Today's Prayer

5

Love: Living in Peace and Safety

But all who listen to me shall live in peace and safety, unafraid.
—Proverbs 1:33 (TLB)

Lady Wisdom asks, "Are you afraid?"

Love provides security. As we grow in our ability to trust Lady Wisdom, living becomes more peaceful and safer. It is not that we do not have difficult situations or trials; the Bible tells us those will come. For the testing of our faith, however, we can go through these times knowing that God is with us. Our confidence is in the wisdom that the Holy Spirit provides. We know that all things work together for our good. With this knowledge, we are less anxious and fearful.

The Bible says that perfect love casts out all fear. Fear has to go when love is in the room of our hearts. A loved person can demonstrate and give love because that is what they have stored inside. What is inside must come out.

As parents, we want to provide a safe environment for our children, a peaceful home. That is what Father God provides for us as we grow in godliness. When we get to heaven, we will be saved from all fear because we will be in God's very presence and we will be like Him for we will see Him as He is. Therefore we must develop in love because the very nature and essence of who God is is love. Perfect love casts out all fear.

One of the rewards of developing the characteristics of love is that we can walk in peace and safety, unafraid because we have the voice of Lady Wisdom speaking to us and giving us guidance on the path of life. As Psalm 23 tells us, we do not have to fear evil because Christ's rod and staff comfort us. He prepares a table before us in the presence of our enemies, and He anoints us for the assignments ahead as we eat and drink at His table of knowledge, understanding, and discernment. The results are peace and safety, which are reflected on our faces and make us beautiful.

Prayer
Dear Lord, I want to develop the characteristics of love so I can walk in peace and safety, unafraid. Help me to listen to the voice of Lady Wisdom speaking to me, giving me guidance on the path of life. Amen.

Word of the Day
Security

Personal Meditations

Today's Prayer

6

Love: Wisdom Granted!

For the Lord grants wisdom! His every word is a
treasure of knowledge and understanding.
—Proverbs 2:6 (TLB)

Lady Wisdom asks, "Do you treasure the word of knowledge and understanding?"

Lady Wisdom speaks to all. She is calling us all to hear the Lord's Word. In the Word, there is treasure, which consists of knowledge and understanding. To know something is the first step in the process of being able to understand it and then use it effectively. Do we really know what love is? Do we understand the love's power? Do we know how to use it and handle love with respect so we can get the full value or treasure found in love?

The wisdom to develop the character of love in ways that bring remarkable rewards must show up in our works. The book of James states that faith without works is dead. Our works are how nonbelieving people will know about Jesus Christ and His love by our deeds and acts of love. We need wisdom too so we do not misapply the concepts of good works, which can be defined as a person's actions or deeds.

When we look at love as a tool to discover the treasure of knowledge and understanding, then we can look at people as hidden treasure. There is that treasure (knowledge and understanding) hidden in us, and first we must use love to excavate it. What is it that is in us? What Word of God has been buried in us that needs to be revealed? Jesus commanded us to love the Lord your God and to love your neighbor as you love yourself.

If we do not love ourselves, how can we love others and help them to find the treasure in themselves?

Prayer
Dear Lord, Please grant us wisdom! Amen.

Word of the Day
Treasure

Personal Meditations

Today's Prayer

7

Love: Response of Love

He grants good sense to the godly—his saints. He is their
shield, protecting them and guarding their pathway. He
shows how to distinguish right from wrong, how to find the
right decision every time. For wisdom and truth will enter
the very center of your being, filling your life with joy.
—Proverbs 2:7–10 (TLB)

Lady Wisdom asks, "How do you respond to the love that is in you for another?"

God responded to His love for us by deciding to be our shield, protector, guard, guide, and counselor, to make sure we are not alone. He even decided to enter our heart, the very center of our beings depositing joy! The Lord really added value to our lives, enhancing His love inside of us.

Our response to God's love should be to do the same for others. The characteristics of love are manifested in whom we become for others. We are then able to be a shield, protector, guard, guide, and counselor for others. To walk in the pathway of righteousness presents the opportunity to navigate the world with the assurance that we are adding value.

When one receives a grant or an endowment of good sense, then there is the expectation that it will be used in the best way possible. The characteristics of love will ensure that the person who has God's approval will use it to enrich the kingdom agenda.

The true power of love is found in unselfish attitudes and generous actions that look for the best for another person without expecting something in return. Wisdom and truth assist with the transformation of our mind-sets, thus propelling us into becoming Christ-like. Our lives become joyful and full of meaning and purpose.

Prayer

Dear Lord, I want to experience the true power of love. Help me to become unselfish with a grateful attitude. Make me generous in my actions. Transform my mind-set to be like Yours. Amen.

Word of the Day
Respond

Personal Meditations

Today's Prayer

8

Love: Good Judgment

The man who knows right from wrong and has good
judgement and common sense is happier than the man who
is immensely rich! For such wisdom is far more valuable
than precious jewels. Nothing else compares with it.
—Proverbs 3:13–15 (TLB)

Lady Wisdom asks, "What is making you happy?"

Looking at immense riches from the lens of love will make one examine what is and is not most important. I do admit that being financially secure is something I want to be. Money can solve a lot of problems. However, I do not want money to be the driving factor of why I do the things I do. There has to be a moral compass that determines my motivation to act on things. Love must be the lens in which every action is derived from.

Jesus commands that we love one another. So the pursuit of love must take first place in our life. Knowing right from wrong and having good judgment and common sense will empower us to make sound and good decisions that benefit ourselves as well as others. The commandment to love is basic to all wisdom. Wisdom is a given value because when we perform acts of love toward others, we are happier. Happiness is a by-product of love. The pursuit of love produces acts of joy, which in turn rewards us with happiness.

A happy person is very attractive. They tend to have a smile on their faces. They're relaxed and welcoming. They are approachable and giving. They make you feel safe, at least for the moment that you are with them because you know they will not do you any harm. That is attractive!

Good judgment and common sense make one aware of others' needs. One becomes sensitive to what does and does not work. As we pursue Jesus's love, we will find in His words the way to go about loving others. Wisdom will inform us of how to handle situations that require us to use good judgment and common sense in a loving way. Jesus's love becomes a well from which we can draw from when we need to love others. We are rich!

Prayer
Dear Lord, Help me to have good judgment and common sense. Make me aware of others' needs. I want to become sensitive to what does and does not work. Amen.

Word of the Day
Wisdom

Personal Meditations

Today's Prayer

9

Love: Wisdom and Common Sense

Have two goals: wisdom—that is, knowing and doing right—
and common sense. Don't let them slip away, for they fill you
with living energy, and are a feather in your cap. They keep you
safe from defeat and disaster and from stumbling off the trail.
—Proverbs 3:21–23 (TLB)

Lady Wisdom asks, "Are you getting your energy from love?"

Wisdom and common sense give you energy. Have you ever wanted
to do something for someone else that required you go the extra mile?
You wondered where you would get the energy to do it. However when
you focused on the person, your love took over, and you were able to
overcome exhaustion, that feeling of overtiredness, low energy, and the
strong desire to sleep. Love created the energy you needed to complete
the desired result.

Love motivated Jesus Christ. He loved us so much that He was willing
to put aside His position to save us from our sin. The Bible says that
He took on the role of a servant. He became poor so we could become
rich in Christ. He was wounded for us so we could have a personal
relationship with Father God. Jesus went the extra mile.

The way to overcome our lack of energy is to gain wisdom from God
so we can move forward with good understanding or revelation of what
needs to be done. We can ask the question, "Does this make sense? Will
it help or hinder?" The living energy that will assist us is ours for the
asking so we do not have to live a defeated life. We will have the energy
to fulfill our dreams.

Prayer

Dear Lord, Help me to seek out wisdom and common sense in every task I attempt to do. Help me to have the patience to listen and learn. Amen.

Word of the Day
Motivation

Personal Meditations

Today's Prayer

10

Love: Cling to Wisdom

Cling to wisdom—she will protect you.
Love her—she will guard you.
—Proverbs 4:6 (TLB)

Lady Wisdom asks, "Do you love me?"

In Proverbs 4, a mentor speaks to the young men and tells them to listen to him as they would listen to their father. By listening, it states that they would grow in wisdom. He tells them that he is trustworthy and would not lie to them. He lets them know that he too was a son loved by his parents. He was their only child. His father must have been a wise man because he took the time to share his wisdom with his son. He gave him wise advice that the father believed would give him success in life. He wanted his son to have a "long and happy life." "Learn to be wise," he said, "and develop good judgement and common sense!" (Proverbs 4:5 TLB). I cannot overemphasize this point.

The mentor wanted the young men to value wisdom and spoke of her as a protector and a guard. Lady Wisdom is a warrior woman. She is strong and has the ability to protect and defend those who follow her words and ways. Lady Wisdom has a love that is not superficial but is powerful, like a lioness caring for her cubs. However, she demands commitment and loyalty.

Determination is the characteristic that we need to be able to cling to and love wisdom. It is called the first step toward becoming wise. Common sense is also needed to accompany determination, along with good judgment. Clinging to wisdom has its rewards. Recognizing wisdom in decision-making enables one to avoid the pitfalls of life and love. People will notice your character because it will be established on love, a love for wisdom. Honor is the by-product of loving wisdom, even to the level of becoming the king or CEO with a long, good life.

Prayer
Dear Lord, Please give me the determination to follow through with what wisdom is telling me to do. I want to recognize Your wise advice in every decision I need to make so I can avoid the dangers of life. Amen.

Word of the Day
Determination

Personal Meditations

Today's Prayer

11

Love: Real Living

But the good man walks along in the ever brightening light
of God's favor, the dawn gives way to morning splendor,
while the evil man gropes and stumbles in the dark.
—Proverbs 4:18 (TLB)

Lady Wisdom asks, "Are you being led to real living?"

What is real living? Our society would tell us that real living is living to gain a lot of money and states. However, is this real living? After one amasses a large sum of money, then what? In Luke 16:12-21, the Bible tells of a man who made a huge amount of money or resources and then decided to build bigger barns to store them in. To his misfortune, his soul was demanded that day, and he died, leaving all of his riches behind.

The rich, young ruler is another story in Luke 18:18–30 where Jesus told him to sell off his wealth and give it to the poor and follow Him. Giving up his wealth was too much for him to do. Saddened, he turned away from Jesus and did not follow Him.

Love requires that we be givers. The Bible also says, "For what is a man profited, if he shall gain the whole world, and lose his own soul? Or what shall a man give in exchange for his soul?" (Matthew 16:26). I like how the Contemporary English Version states the verse, "What will you gain, if you won the whole world but destroy yourself? What would you give to get back your soul?"

Lady Wisdom will lead you to real living. Real living is serving God by serving others with love.

Prayer
Dear Lord, I want to experience real living. Help me to serve others with love. Amen.

Word of the Day
Real Living

Personal Meditations

Today's Prayer

Developing the Source of

JOY

12

Joy: Blessing of Joyfulness

A cheerful heart does good like medicine,
but a broken spirit makes one sick.
—Proverbs 17:22 (TLB)

Lady Wisdom asks, "Is joy settled in your heart?"

I want to do whatever I must do from a heart of joy. That way, my work or anything I do is coming from a heart of love and no obligation. When I feel I am obligated to do things, then it feels like I am toiling, and there is no enjoyment in the process. It makes it difficult to appreciate the process. I want whatever I do to come from a motivation of joyfulness.

1 Thessalonians 5:18 says, "In all things give thanks ..." However, it is hard to give thanks for things we do not value. We must see the value in the learning. What am I going to gain from this activity? How will it assist me in my growth? I want to rise to a new level of maturity. Having the feeling of weariness and fatigue does not promote enthusiasm for the activity or work.

Matthew 12:34 says, "Out of the abundance of the heart the mouth speaks." If there is no joy in my heart for what I am doing, then I need to not do it. It is because I would not be speaking life into the thing I am trying to produce. There is power in our thoughts and words. That is why we need to have enjoyable ideas that will deliver the speech that is joyful and then acceptable actions full of joy. Having the right heart's disposition by knowing why we are doing the things that we do and then making sure it is from a spirit of joy will produce success every time.

Prayer

Dear Lord, Help me to have the confidence and settled assurance that God is in control of all the details of my life so I can do things for others with a joyful heart. Amen.

Word of the Day
Joyfulness

Personal Meditations

Today's Prayer

13.

Joy: Guard Your Affections

Above all else, guard your affections. For they influence everything else in your life.

—Proverbs 4:23 (TLB)

Lady Wisdom asks, "Who stole your joy?"

If you were to ask people what they want out of life, their answer would probably be, "I want to be happy." That statement has a lot of hidden meaning to it. In our constitution, it speaks of the "pursuit of happiness." It depicts happiness as something to strive for rather than to be. How does one pursue happiness? What is the definition of happiness, and who said the definition is correct?

Lady Wisdom implies that your affections—which I am defining as joy—can be stolen or taken away from your life. I do not want to mix up the two, happiness and joy. Happiness, to me, is a feeling that one gets because of a situation. It is dependent on the atmosphere around it. It is also limited to an experience or object.

Joy, on the other hand, is a state of being and can be found in Jesus. Jesus gives joy. Salvation produces joy. A relationship with God promises joy in every situation and circumstance. It is not predicated on what is happening, but on the presence of the Holy Spirit directing our lives.

That puts joy in a whole different level of understanding. Joy can be nurtured and developed. It can be the lens in which we see the world—through the lens of joy. Jesus's joy can influence how we deal with life's trials and experiences. Jesus promised us joy. Joy is found in the Old and New Testaments. Joy is what we get to have when we become a part of God's kingdom, which is righteousness, peace, and joy in the Holy Ghost. The joy of the Lord is your strength. We can have a life of joy!

Prayer

Dear Lord, Help me to be focus on You and the joy You provide each day. I want to experience Your joy every morning, knowing You have great things in store for me. Amen.

Word of the Day
Affections

Personal Meditations

Today's Prayer

14

Joy: Drink from Your Own Well

> Drink from your own well, my son—
> be faithful and true to your wife.
> —Proverbs 5:15

Lady Wisdom asks, "Where are you finding your happiness?"

Jesus Christ promised the woman at the well that water could quench her soul. She was drinking from the emotional well of sexual and emotional temporal gratification. It was meeting her need to be loved and appreciated for a moment but was not lasting. This need for happiness led her down a path of pain because she ended up losing her respect, her own moral compass, and her ability to love herself. She had been drinking from five other men's wells, and the man she was now living with was not even her husband. She was not satisfied.

Jesus came along and offered her water, a different kind of satisfaction. He offered her Jesus joy. She found out that Jesus's joy was not limited, but was a well springing up that could fulfill her thirst for meaning and happiness but could meet the needs of her community too.

Jesus joy allows us to be faithful. Faithfulness is who God is, and His faithfulness is great! We can depend on Jesus to be with us. We have confidence in His love for us, like a faithful husband for his beloved bride. Therefore we are able to relax in His love and drink of His water, finding the contentment and happiness that only He can provide. Our King Jesus, or Husband, sits at the throne of our heart. We love Him. Our relationship with Jesus allows us to achieve joy that is not dependent on wealth and circumstances. We can temporarily build happiness into our lives by adopting certain behaviors and attitudes like discipline, good habits, meditation, and positive thinking. However, to receive the full benefits of joy, we must cultivate a spiritual relationship with the Creator, the one who made us and the one whom we were designed to give glory.

Joy offers a permanent spiritual change of heart, mind, and emotions. The Holy Spirit cultivates the spirit of joy when we pursue and strive to develop the spirit of joy by following the Lord Jesus. The Lord commands our attention and affections as we go all out for happiness in Him. We are rewarded with an indescribable encounter of joy from the love of Jesus Christ.

Prayer
Dear Lord, Help me to find my joy in my home and with my loved ones. First, let me cultivate the spirit of joy in my own heart with You. Amen.

Word of the Day
Faithfulness

Personal Meditations

Today's Prayer

15

Joy: God's Constant Delight

I was his constant delight, laughing and playing in his presence.
And how happy I was with what he created—his wide world
and all his family of mankind! And so young men, listen to
me, for how happy are all who follow my instructions.
—Proverbs 8:30–32 (TLB)

Lady Wisdom asks, "How happy are you?"

God takes pleasure in the prospering of His people. He made us to give Him joy. Lady Wisdom fulfilled a longing from God to give joy. She responded to His creation with laughter and delight. She was genuinely happy and showed it. She knew what gave God wanted most of all, a family.

We have an opportunity to be a part of the family of God. We too can receive a lot of joy from our heavenly Father. We can experience great joy when we make Jesus the king of our hearts. From our hearts will flow exuberant joy. The Holy Spirit will teach us the way to obtain supernatural joy that in every situation we will be able to be content. Our lives will not be dictated by emotions of happiness, but by the divine power of joy.

Joy also is a response to God's creative power. When we do the Father's will, He affirms our actions. Satisfaction fills us. His approval brings joy. We have completed the instructions that Lady Wisdom gave us. Our life's purpose has meaning. Finding the real joy opens us up for a creative flow, like our Father.

God has given us the ability to create happy experiences in our lives, which can give us contentment. These experiences can come through behaviors and attitudes, such as discipline, good habits, positive mindset, mediation, and passion. However, the foundation of our joy must come from a deep relationship with Father God. As we find joy in Him, then we can be satisfied.

Prayer
Dear Lord, Help me not to take Your joy for granted. I want to see what You see and enjoy what You enjoy. Amen.

Word of the Day
Contentment

Personal Meditations

Today's Prayer

16

Joy: Watching Daily for Lady Wisdom

Happy is the man who is so anxious, to be with me that he watches
for me daily at my gates, or waits for me outside my home! For
whoever finds me finds life and wins approval from the Lord.
—Proverbs 8:34–35 (TLB)

Lady Wisdom asks, "Have you missed me today?"

Lady Wisdom is eagerly willing to give great counsel to whoever wants
it. She commands us to listen and be wise. There is joy in following her
advice because the Lord approves it. There is divine recognition in our
ability to obey the voice of wisdom. God's approval rewards our efforts.

Finding that place in us that is anxious for the Lord and wisdom
produces joy. What revelation will I receive today that will help me to
prosper in my life? Each day the revelation is fresh and provides ways
for self-improvement. This process helps us to serve others and God with
authenticity. We become more fulfilled. Therefore, we feel and see the
joy rising in our lives. We can ride the waves of joy!

Our lives become infused with joy. The beauty of deep, abiding
contentment shows up in our attitude with ourselves and others. We
are not reactionary but proactive in producing beauty and beautiful
moments. We have moments of salvation where we are freed from things
that would have brought us down into despair. We are now lifted into
happiness and ultimately joy!

Prayer
Dear Lord, I want to establish a close relationship with Lady Wisdom
so I can experience the joy of the Lord every day. Amen.

Word of the Day
Watching

Personal Meditations

Today's Prayer

17

Joy: Right Living and Lasting Happiness

Ill-gotten gain brings no lasting happiness; right living does.
—Proverbs 10:2 (TLB)

Lady Wisdom asks, "How are you living?"

Right living is the foundation to lasting happiness. Pray first and then act. Spending time in prayer leads to revelation, which will give the inspiration to do what needs to be done. Prayer brings joy. When we pray about what we are inspired to do, then we do not work by impulse but by faith. We are in a position of humility. God gives grace to the humble.

Anxiety leads to impulsive actions, which then leads to manipulation. When we try to manipulate the situation and be controlling, it sets up an unhappy place in our hearts. Frustration sets in, and we start to think negative thoughts about people. Trust cannot live in this environment. Haste makes waste!

Seeking wisdom in prayer allows God to work on our behalf. There is a comforting joy in knowing that God has our back and He wants us to succeed. Our job is to stop, pray, and ask for wisdom. God has the master plan, and we have to depend on Him to release the blueprint into our hands so we can move according to His will. We need the Holy Spirit to provide the next steps. It is a faith walk.

Prayer
Dear Lord, Help me to be honest with myself that joy is not about doing things for temporal success but rather my lasting joy comes from following You. Amen.

Word of the Day
Foundation

Personal Meditations

Today's Prayer

18

Joy: Happy Memories, Good Name

We all have happy memories of good men gone to their
reward, but the names of wicked men stink after them.
—Proverbs 10:7 (TLB)

Lady Wisdom asks, "Who are the good men or women in your life?"

We all love to recall happy memories of people who impacted our lives.
Their influence helped us to see the world and navigate it in a productive
manner. These people reminded us of our value and that anything is
possible if we have the faith to believe. At this moment, I am thinking
about my father, Joseph, who was a good man and I know has gone to
his reward. When I recall how he used to hug me tight and call me "my
beautiful daughter," I have a warm feeling of love and acceptance from
him. I knew that my father loved me and that he would be there for me
if I needed help. It was very comforting to have him as my safety net.
His life has left a sweet aroma in many lives as they think about my
father's kindness. Joy fills me.

There have been wicked men or women in my life; however, because of
wisdom, I have been able to avoid them and actually forget about them.
The thoughts of them stink. The Holy Spirit has a way of removing these
people and thoughts and putting them into the sea of forgetfulness.
What a blessing!

How can we learn from these people? Creating happy memories for the
people whom we want to influence is one way of leaving joyful memories.
Another way is saying joy-filled words and positive affirmations, which
will leave images of joy. Words have power to give life. Serving others

with the right motives will also leave a positive impression on the community and build a legacy that smells sweet, leaving a joyful aroma.

Prayer
Dear Lord, Help me to have the right motives in serving You. I want to leave a sweet, joyful aroma of Your glory whenever people think about me. Amen.

Word of the Day
Memories

Personal Meditations

Today's Prayer

19

Joy: Joyful to Have Instructions

The wise man is glad to be instructed, but, a self-
sufficient fool falls flat on his face.
—Proverbs 10:8 (TLB)

Lady Wisdom asks, "Is your autonomy and self-reliance worth falling flat on your face?"

Have you ever been stuck and you just needed the right instructions so you could finish an assignment? When someone takes the time to tell you what to do, a sense of relief showers over you, and then you are able to focus. The task becomes simple, and an eagerness to complete the job takes over. You can't wait to finish the assignment.

There are times when being self-reliant appears the way to go. However, a huge roadblock is ahead. The warning signs are there, but you refuse to stop and notice them. You may even have someone who is telling you to stop and do it another way. Yet you are not willing to give what they have to say a second chance. The end result is that your desire for autonomy leads you down a path of failure. Therefore, you fall flat on your face.

Receiving instructions from an advisor or a trusted friend is the sign of a wise man or woman. Being able to stop and consider all sides to a problem and/or look at different solutions demonstrates a level of wisdom and maturity. Counting the cost is golden. The rewards will bring great joy in the long run.

Prayer

Dear Lord, I need You every moment of my life. Help me to see You speaking through others and be able to receive the word of the Lord with joy. Amen.

Word of the Day
Receiving

Personal Meditations

Today's Prayer

20

Joy: Eternal Happiness

The hope of good men is eternal happiness;
the hopes of evil men are all in vain.
—Proverbs 10:28 (TLB)

Lady Wisdom asks, "What are you hoping for, and will it last?"

The idea of eternal happiness is very attractive. Who does not want to experience happiness? Our constitution provides us the right to pursue happiness; therefore I believe that happiness is something that people want. Many people are surrounded with things that may make them happy. But can it give them lasting and eternal joy?

I like this definition of happiness. Happiness is about what happens to you. It is dependent on your circumstances, behavior, and attitudes. Joy takes on a deeper meaning because it is dependent on a personal relationship with the Creator God. This places happiness into the realm of the eternal and the supernatural, where God is. The good man or woman has hope. In contrast, the evil man or woman hopes in vain. Goodness versus evil determines one's eternal happiness.

To obtain eternal happiness, there must be a pursuit of goodness or following the path of doing well. The good woman's life is filled with joy and the beauty of deep, abiding contentment because of the lifestyle of goodness. Goodness produces hope, which in turn results in eternal happiness. Hope in God makes joy possible for eternity.

Prayer
Dear Lord, My hope is in You. Please help me to lean on You and Your Word for my joy. My eternal happiness is in You. Amen.

Word of the Day
Happiness

Personal Meditations

Today's Prayer

21

Joy: Celebrating a Good Man

The whole city celebrates a good man's success—
and also the godless man's death.
—Proverbs 11:10 (TLB)

Lady Wisdom asks, "Who will be at your funeral?"

Let's celebrate the accomplishments of a good man or woman. When my father passed away, he was celebrated in the city of Boston and also on the island of Montserrat. My father was dedicated to God and the church. He assisted the church in many ways, and the most outstanding accomplishment was organizing the church's fundraising to burn the church mortgage. He wanted the house of the Lord to be debt-free.

In Montserrat, my father shepherded his church during the time of the volcanic eruptions that caused many people to flee to the United States and England. He decided to stay and help the people who had nowhere to go but to the northern side of the island. He converted the church into a shelter for the homeless. He advocated for the people with the British government. Because of his faithfulness and dedication, many people received aid and resources during that trying time.

At his death, the people honored him by having three days of celebration as his body lay in state. Many came from neighboring islands to pay their respects. On the day of his funeral, the island shut down for at least a half-day. His funeral was heard on the radio.

To have others remember you and celebrate your life, we must serve others. Joy is related to thankfulness. Our lives will be celebrated with joy because people will want to show their gratitude for a life well lived. What do you want to be remembered for?

Prayer
Dear Lord, I want my life to have great meaning and purpose so others will be blessed. Amen.

Word of the Day
Celebrate

Today's Prayer

22

Joy: The Lord's Delight

The Lord hates the stubborn but delights in those who are good.
—Proverbs 11:26 (TLB)

Lady Wisdom asks, "Do you want to give the Lord some joy?"

I love the song written by Jonathan Nelson entitled "Smile/Better is One Day Medley." He states, "Here is my worship. Take joy in it." Asking God to receive our worship and wanting God to enjoy it changes the dynamic of the relationship. Instead of what you have done for me, rather it is, "What and how can I bless you?"

The Lord hates the stubborn because I believe that they are not trusting Him. It gives God great pleasure when we trust His words. It is like a parent who is happy when their children follow their instructions and are obedient. Obedience from a child gives joy to the parent, teacher, or whoever is caring for them. Stubbornness is a form of rebellion. A rebellious attitude leads to a great fall.

Being a delight to the Lord should be our goal. If our relationship with God is a love relationship, then we should have the desire to please Him. I am not saying that we are perfect but that our motives are right. We do what we do because we want to see the Lord smile. We want to give Him joy.

The way to do that is to spend time with God in prayer and worship. Get to know Him. Understand His ways. That requires making room for God and giving Him our best time of the day. I strongly believe in waking up early in the morning. Robin Sharma calls 5:00 a.m. to 8:00 a.m. the holy hours of the day. He believes these hours are sacred. If that is true, then we need to give that time to the Lord and make Him smile. Amen.

Prayer
Dear Lord, I want to get to know You better. Whenever I become stubborn and unwilling to learn, please remind me of Your love for me. Amen.

Word of the Day
Delight

Personal Meditations

Today's Prayer

Digging the Reservoir of

PEACE

23

Peace: How to Be a Peacemaker

To quarrel with a neighbor is foolish; a man
with good sense holds his tongue.
—Proverbs 11:12 (TLB)

Lady Wisdom asks, "Are you living peaceably with everyone?"

Have you ever been confronted by a person who just wanted to accuse you of something or pick a fight with you? You knew that to respond to this person would only make the matter worse. Yet you knew that you were in the right. The opportunity to prove your point was there, but instead you decided to keep quiet just to "keep the peace." Proverbs calls you a person with good sense because you held your tongue.

Jesus said in John 14:27 when He was departing the earth and returning to His heavenly Father that he was leaving the gift of peace with His disciples. This peace was His peace. He told them that His peace is not like the kind of peace found in the world. The type of peace that He was leaving was "perfect peace." That is the kind of peace that the world is looking for today.

The idea of being a peacemaker reflects what Jesus gave us, peace. He also said that if we are peacemakers, then we will be called the "Sons of God." Working toward peaceful solutions is a noble thing to do. We even give awards to people who look for peaceful ways to enhance goodness on the planet. It is called the Nobel Peace Prize. The apostle Paul said in Romans 12:18 that if it is possible, to live peaceably with all men.

So the question is: How do we become a peacemaker? We must be determined to follow the way of peace. First, we cannot react to every comment or action that rubs us the wrong way. We must stop, think, and then respond. This proverb gives us the solution to keeping the peace: do not quarrel with your neighbor and then hold your tongue!

Prayer
Dear Lord, Help me to be quiet and hold my tongue when someone is doing or saying something that is offensive. Help me to be a peacemaker. Amen.

Word of the Day
Peaceable

Personal Meditations

Today's Prayer

24

Peace: Promoting Peace

Deceit fills hearts that are plotting for evil, joy
fills hearts that are planning for good!
—Proverbs 12:20 (TLB)

Lady Wisdom asks, "What is in your heart, plotting evil or promoting joy?"

The opposite of planning for good is plotting for evil. Which one are you concentrating on? When we take offense to what someone has done to us, then we find ourselves thinking of ways to get the person back for what they have done to us. It is a very dark place to be and can lead to every kind of evil.

People who promote peace have joy! Experiencing a life of peace is walking with Jesus. Jesus is the Prince of Peace. What is in your heart will come out. Therefore we must cultivate a spirit of peace. We can do this by following the instructions of the Holy Spirit.

We can achieve peace by making it a part of our mission and doing the work required to make it happen. Letting other distractions keep us from a lifestyle of peace can make us worry and become weary. Taking that deep breath and calling on the name of the Lord Jesus is the means to move in peace.

God's peace is the key to an amazing life. Let us do what He says and continue to desire what He wants for us. Keep on asking and looking for ways to promote peace.

Prayer
Dear Lord, I want to be a promoter of peace. Teach me how to plan for what You want on this earth. Help me to live a lifestyle of peace. Amen.

Word of the Day
Promote

Personal Meditations

Today's Prayer

25

Peace: Pleasing God Leads to Peace

When a man is trying to please God, God makes even
his worst enemies to be at peace with him.
—Proverbs 16:7 (TLB)

Lady Wisdom asks, "Is the Lord taking pleasure in how you act?"

Do you have peace with God? It all starts with Him. The apostle
Paul writes, "Therefore, having been justified by faith, we have peace
with God through our Lord Jesus Christ" (Romans 5:1 KJV). Our
relationship with God has changed because of our union with Jesus.
We are one with Christ; therefore peace is part of our nature. We are
now a part of the family of God. As a loving Father God, He is happy
with our efforts to follow His way of doing and being. When a man's
ways please God, He works to make good things happen for us because
He is a good Father.

I find that sometimes I look for peace in the wrong places. Trying to
find peace in other people by putting my trust in them only leads to
disappointment. People cannot give you peace. We end up creating
enemies because we are offended by the behaviors of the ones we thought
should give us peace.

How do we find the peace we are looking for? Jesus is the peacemaker.
He is the one who can give us the strategies we need to develop a peace
plan. When we follow His ways of being and doing things, we will be
able to live in peace with God and our enemies. Lady Wisdom will
expose us to the understanding and insights of how to win over people.
We will gain discernment of what to do and not do at the right time.

There will be nothing to complain about because we will be able to create a win-win situation. Everyone will be able to agree.

Prayer
Dear Lord, I know You have all the answers I need to be able to have peace with my enemies. Help me to look past my own bias and instead look at Your peaceful ways of bringing people together. Amen.

Word of the Day
Strategies

Personal Meditations

Today's Prayer

26

Peace: How to Kill a Friendship

An evil man sows strife; gossip parts the best of friends.
—Proverbs 16:28 (TLB)

Lady Wisdom asks, "Are you going to listen to the gossiper or me?"

How to kill a friendship is to listen to the wrong voices. Evil people have only one intention, to see everything go their way. They have no desire to make other people's lives better. If they see the possibility of you getting ahead, then they will interrupt that by saying just the meanest thing to stop you in your tracks.

Losing a trusted best friend can be a very difficult experience. If we only knew how powerful our words are, we would be a little more careful in what we say to each other. Evil men with selfish ambitions have a way of saying the things that only benefit themselves and not the people whom they claim to love.

Peace and harmony in any relationship can bring great success. When there is agreement, things happen. Two are stronger than one. If two people are determined to accomplish a task, there is nothing that can stop them, other than themselves. Getting into the position of offense can hinder any attempts at reconciliation. That is why in relationships it is important to pay attention to the voices that are speaking. What is the motive for their comments? Is there some truth to it? If so, how can it be used to improve and enhance the progress or relationship?

Thankfully, love is a more powerful force. Love can work and fix the situation. God is love. If God has a different plan, then He will intervene and set things straight. We just have to keep on praying and depending on Him.

Prayer
Dear Lord, Thank You for being a God of peace. Increase my ability to hear and pay attention to the right voices. Help me to not become offended by the comments made that can destroy my friendship with the people I love. Amen.

Word of the Day
Friendship

Personal Meditations

Today's Prayer

27

Peace: Your Bad Temper Gets Nowhere

A short-tempered man must bear his own penalty; you can't do
much to help him. If you try once you must try a dozen times!
—Proverbs 19:17 TLB

Lady Wisdom asks, "Is your temper costing you many friends,
opportunities, and money?"

Being aware of your feelings at any given time is necessary in certain situations.
We must discover our triggers and stop before we judge a situation. People
experience these feelings of anger because there is a self-control problem.
Something or someone is getting away from them, and feelings of anxiety
overtake them. We have to remember that we cannot control other people.
God has given each one of us a mind of our own. We are our own CEO.
Therefore, each individual has to choose to conform to the situation.

The fruit of peace begins in the inside of an individual. Which triggers
cause the anger to rise? Looking deep within the past and also relationships
with important people can unmask the hidden hurts and pains that
cause anger. Are there experiences of abandonment, neglect, or abuse?

To remain at peace, it is wise to not get involved with people who have a
short-temper. Lady Wisdom tells us that we cannot do much to help them.
They have to experience the results of their actions, and maybe then they
may change. It is not guaranteed. On the other hand, if you want to help
a person with a bad temper, then get ready to develop the fruit of patience!

Prayer
Dear Lord, Help me to assess my triggers and not become short-
tempered or bitter. I want to maintain my peace. Amen.

Word of the Day
Assessment

Personal Meditations

Today's Prayer

28

Peace: Crust of Bread or Steak?

A dry crust eaten in peace is better than steak
every day along with argument and strife.
—Proverbs 17:1 (TLB)

Lady Wisdom asks, "How is your health?"

Sometimes it is necessary to get away just to have some peace. We all crave a level of balance and equilibrium. Living in a situation where there is never a quiet, peaceful moment can and will affect a person's health. We cannot survive in continual chaos. The mind and body will soon burn out.

We have choices! Deciding to stay amongst argument and strife can bring pain and harm to the body, mind/emotions, and spirit. Getting away each morning in a sacred space helps to bring a balance to mind. We can consult with God, and He will give us the needed covering to protect our minds from overload. The Bible states in Isaiah 59:19 (KJV), "So shall they fear the name of the LORD from the west, and his glory from the rising of the sun. When the enemy shall come in like a flood, the Spirit of the LORD shall lift up a standard against him." The Word of God will be a shield of protection.

The keys of prayer and attitude of gratitude will change the situation around. Let the argument and strife lead you to the cross, the blood, and the comfort of Jesus. What I mean by that is if we focus on Jesus and tell Him our concerns, then He will release answers and a way of escape. His glorious light will shine and bring peace.

Prayer
Dear Lord, Help me to remember that I have a quiet place in You. You will help me if I cultivate peace. Amen.

Word of the Day
Necessary Space

Personal Meditations

Today's Prayer

29

Peace: How to Stop a Quarrel

It is hard to stop a quarrel once it starts, so don't let it begin.
—Proverbs 17:14 (TLB)

Lady Wisdom asks, "Do you have the ability to be quiet?"

Many times it is tempting to participate in an argument, especially if you are right. The need to be heard can override common sense. Getting the upper hand may happen in the beginning, but there can be negative consequences in the future.

Lady Wisdom tells us to be quiet! Let it pass and you will win the war without even opening your mouth. The question is, "Do you have the self-control to be silent?" I like what Hebrews 12:11 (AMP) says, "For the time being no discipline brings joy, but seems sad and painful yet to those who have been trained by it, afterwards it yields the peaceful fruit of righteousness" [right standing with God and a lifestyle and attitude that seeks conformity to God's will and purpose].

I think that cultivating a lifestyle built on a positive attitude will attract the environment of reason and a positive mind-set. A wise stand will become useful in times of argument and strife. It will position us for overcoming the destructive words and attempts of negative forces to destroy our peace. Silence is golden!

Prayer
Dear Lord, I need You to speak in my ear when I want to defend myself. Help me to remember that You will take care of the situation. Help me to be silent. Amen.

Word of the Day
Quiet

Personal Meditations

Today's Prayer

30

Peace: Stay Out of Danger

A fool gets into constant fights. His mouth is
his undoing! His words endanger him.
—Proverbs 18:6–7 (TLB)

Lady Wisdom asks, "Who hurt you?"

When a person is getting into fights all of the time, then there has to be some underlying reason for the foolish behavior. Something from the past has that person stuck in a web of confusion. For some reason, they are not able to hear or see the good in any situation. Some event or experience in their past has clouded their emotional and spiritual vision.

This is a very serious problem because ultimately it can cause great harm to the individual and anyone associated with them. Getting into constant fights will expose them to other fools who might even be more foolish than they are. He can also become so angry that it leads to extreme violence and the consequence of death.

It is important that a person with these issues seeks professional help. The professional will be able to help them discover what the underlying issue is and bring some clarity to the problem. Prayer is also needed that the person will be protected by his foolishness and have a change of heart. The heart of this person can be touched and changed by the Holy Spirit. God's grace and mercy are available. Amen!

Prayer
Dear Lord, Please have mercy and bring clarity concerning the causes of this foolish behavior. Give us wisdom to see the answer. Amen.

Word of the Day
Clarity

Personal Meditations

Today's Prayer

31

Peace: Overlooking Insults
Equals Blessings

A wise man restrains his anger and overlooks
insults. This is to his credit.
—Proverbs 19:11 (TLB)

Lady Wisdom asks, "Are you able to overlook the insults and get to the heart of the matter?"

Sometimes when a person is insulting you, it is because they have underlying issues that are causing them to not think straight. Their anger is not really about you. It may be about a reoccurring issue they have not dealt with. Somehow, whatever you said or did triggered a negative response.

Giving yourself the advantage of wait time makes you a wise person. That moment to think and assess the situation can give you the opportunity to respond the appropriate way. It can lead to a positive outcome. You may be able to do or say something that can bring peace to the situation.

Wisdom is great to ask for in those times of uncertainty. Even in the process of asking, it is enough time to gain some insight before responding. Wisdom tells us to get understanding. Getting the deeper meaning of what is going on can give you the best outcome. For it is with common sense and good judgment that will allow you to restrain your anger and overlook the insults for a better solution.

Prayer
Dear Lord, Thank You for helping me to grow in wisdom and understanding so I can keep quiet and wait for the correct response to difficult situations. Amen.

Word of the Day
Wait Time

Personal Meditations

Today's Prayer

32

Peace: Drip! Drip! Drip!

A rebellious son is a calamity to his father and a
nagging wife annoys like constant dripping.
—Proverbs 19:13 (TLB)

Lady Wisdom asks, "Where is the leadership in the household?"

Rebellion and discontent happen when people are not being fulfilled in a relationship. A rebel is defined as a person who rises up in opposition or resistance against the ruling authority. They are in defiance to the authority in their house. Their refusal to obey orders and be a cooperative member of the family may be because of a lack of discipline, training, and time spent with the father. A nagging wife is a discontent woman who wants her husband's attention. She does not feel that she is being heard; therefore she responds by verbalizing her concerns. In the end, it sounds like nagging. She becomes annoying, and her husband really doesn't listen, therefore increasing the drip!

These types of behaviors make the household a very chaotic place to live in because you do not know what will happen next. Rebellion and continual nagging and harassing behaviors can bring instability to the environment. The hot-bloodedness and explosiveness may be demonstrated in impulsive actions. The wife's nagging reveals a grievous and disgruntled feeling of the prevailing situation in her household. There is no peace or predictability in the family because these behaviors can become tormenting and grievous.

Everyone needs a peaceful place to call home. Having a family meeting to air out the issues hovering over each family member may bring relief to the discontent that each person is acting out. The father will need to have a good listening ear, allowing each individual to express themself without judgment. Lady Wisdom suggests that he will have to restrain himself and overlook the insults that may present itself in the discussion because insults will probably come out loud and clear. However, listening to each person's concerns is a step in the right direction because hopefully a solution can be formulated to ease the tension in the household. Prayer is the key that can open up the hearts of each member to be able to change their mind-set and bring lasting peace.

Prayer
Dear Lord, Change the hearts of each person to have a desire for peace. Amen.

Word of the Day
Home

Establishing the Supply of

GOODNESS

33

Goodness: Generosity

It is possible to give away and become richer! It is also possible
to hold on to tightly and lose everything. Yes, the liberal
man shall be rich! By watering others, he waters himself.
—Proverbs 11:24–25 (TLB)

Lady Wisdom asks, "What are you afraid of losing that you cannot give freely?"

In the garden, water is an essential part of the process of growing plants. If the plants do not receive water, then they are going to die. So in the natural and so in the spiritual, when we water others with our time, talent, and treasure, then individuals will live and flourish. In the process of watering others, Proverbs tells us that we water ourselves. The garden of our soul gets watered too! Therefore, we cannot be stingy with the water for the plants or the water of our resources: time, talent, and treasure. Liberality leads to prosperity!

How many people have a rainy-day fund? Our society tells us that we need to hold on to what we have and save for a rainy day. We tend to want to put away for something that may come up unexpectedly. However, this thought can deter us from giving to others. We could start to develop the "what about me" attitude. Hoarding things and not sharing because of fear of not having enough starts to set in.

I am not saying that we should not be prepared for the winter. Proverbs tells us to be like the ant. "Take a lesson from the ants, you lazy fellow. Learn from their ways and be wise. For though they have no king to make them work, yet they labor hard all summer, gathering food for the winter" (Proverbs 6:6–8 TLB).

We need to prepare for the winter season of our lives. Putting away for that time is wise. Having a savings or retirement plan will provide for emergencies and the time when we are unable to work. The resources will be there to cover living expenses.

What I am saying is that it is a blessing to be able to give away when we see someone in need, not to hold back the resources, especially if we have it to give. When we hold on too tightly, then there is the possibility of losing it all to other things. Something will come up to take those same resources away.

The idea of giving away to make you richer is demonstrated with God. He gave away His only begotten Son Jesus, and He became richer with many sons and daughters through Christ. He gained a family. You too can gain an abundance of goodness when you give away too liberally and cheerfully to others. The blessings will find you so you can have more to give.

Prayer
Dear Lord, Please help me to have a heart of generosity so I can water others as I water myself. Amen.

Word of the Day
Freely Give

Personal Meditations

Today's Prayer

34

Goodness: Wonderful Interest

When you help the poor you are lending to the Lord-
and he pays wonderful interest on your loan!
—Proverbs 19:17 (TLB)

Lady Wisdom asks, "How are you strengthening the community?"

When we help the poor, we are really helping ourselves. Have you ever heard the saying that you are as strong as your weakest link? Well, helping the poor to move from poverty to an increasing sense of self-worth is what moves the community forward. Everyone feels better, and hope becomes a force that changes the people's mind-set.

Lending to the Lord does not just mean that you are providing only financial support, but that you are also giving of your voice to issues that affect the moral, spiritual, and harmony of the community. When we speak about what is good and right, then are we acknowledging that there is a divine design that has been constructed before the beginning of time. We are directing our community out of a poverty mind-set and focusing them on the will and purpose of God to prosper us.

God said in the beginning that we are to multiply and replenish the earth. That means we need to be growing our communities out of poverty and into productivity, which will lead to prosperity. The Lord will respond to our generosity by increasing us because He sees our willingness to bless others and to be His hands on the earth.

We help the poor by directing our dollars toward their immediate needs but also by teaching and instructing them on how to expand their thinking from a poverty mind-set to a God-centered mind-set.

Ultimately it is in our relationship with God that we are able to create and then "bloom where we are planted."

Prayer
Dear Lord, Help me not to ignore those who are less fortunate than myself, but to ask You, "How can I serve my community so all can prosper?" Thank You for the answers. Amen.

Word of the Day
Wonderful

Personal Meditations

Today's Prayer

35

Goodness: Giving Ear to the Needy

He who shuts his ears to the cries of the poor
will be ignored in his own time of need.
—Proverbs 21:13 TLB

Lady Wisdom asks, "Why do you ignore the vulnerable and weak among you?"

Jesus Christ, in His ministry on earth, specifically came to change the conditions of the poor and needy. He wanted them to know that they did not have to be poor anymore. The Bible says that Jesus went around doing good. He even fed the people and looked out for their well-being. Ministry to the poor is part of the Christian calling. We are to not overlook the poor.

Something very troubling in our society is the disregard for the less fortunate. The spirit of greed seems to be rising in the places and institutions that were considered to be a support system for the needy. Churches, schools, hospitals, and governments appear to be overtaken by individuals who only see them as ways to make money. It is abusive in nature. These institutions, which used to be people-focused, are now profit-focused and seem to be driven by greed.

I believe that the cries of the poor are rising before the Lord. He is hearing their petitions and looking for those who are willing to do His will to stand up. He is looking for women with the spirit of Deborah and Esther in the land to declare justice. We see the rise of women in all of these institutions deciding to lead the way for the betterment of the community. We all have to ask ourselves this question: "Will we ignore the cries of the poor, or will we take action and do our part to bring healing to our children, youth, and families?"

Prayer
Dear Lord, Give us the voice and strategies to bring about relief to the poor and underserved in our communities. Amen.

Word of the Day
Relief

Personal Meditations

Today's Prayer

36

Goodness: Goodness, the Way to Find Life

The man who tries to be good, loving and kind
finds life, righteousness, and honor.
—Proverbs 21:21TLB

Lady Wisdom asks, "What does it mean to you to be good, loving, and kind?"

Goodness comes from the heart. A person with a heart that is wanting to please God will want to be like God. We know that God is good. It is His nature. If we're going to be like Him, which He told us to do, then we must study how God acts in situations. Goodness is a trait that we must take the time to work out. It requires that we examine our motives and assess our thought toward the situation and people. Ask the question: "Why do we do the things we do? Is it for man's approval, or is it from the heart?"

It is our responsibility to pursue doing things that please God. Treating others with kindness and helping others with acts of goodness will set us apart from others who say they love God and want to follow Him. People will know us by our love. Our acts of generosity will speak for us.

There is a reward for following the ways of God. It is a life that is filled with doing and being right before God, and God, in turn, honors our efforts to be like Him. Just like a father who commends his children for following and doing what he asks, so it is with Father God. He will reward those who seek to please Him.

Prayer

Dear Lord, Help me to set aside my selfish ways and instead desire to do good and kind things for others. I want to naturally respond to others with generosity and kindness so I can find life and right standing with You. I want You to receive the glory for any honor I receive from following Your directions. Thank You for helping me. Amen.

Word of the Day
Kind Things

Personal Meditations

Today's Prayer

37

Goodness: Give and Get Freely

The lazy man longs for many things but his hands refuse to work. He is greedy to get, while the godly love to give!
—Proverbs 21:25–26 (TLB)

Lady Wisdom asks, "Are you a giver?"

This idea of getting something for nothing is so pervasive in our day. What can we get for free? God's love is free, yet we have to cultivate it. There is work involved. There are free opportunities, yet we have to go to them or pursue them. Good effort is the name of the game.

Napoleon Hill in his book *Think and Grow Rich* shared that we have two envelopes that we are all born with. He discussed that these are riches you may enjoy if you take possession of your mind and direct your thoughts to fulfill your own choice. Then there are penalties that you must pay if we neglect to take possession of our thoughts and direct them in the right path. Our riches or blessings are available to each of us, but we must be willing to do the work necessary to obtain them. We are all given sound health, peace of mind, labor of love of your own choice, freedom from fear and worry, positive mental attitude, and material riches of your own choice and quantity. The penalties of neglecting to take possession of one's own mind are ill health, fear and worry, indecision and doubt, frustration and discouragement throughout life, poverty and want, and a whole lot of evil consisting of envy, greed, jealousy, anger, hatred, and superstition.

The thing is that we have the choice to decide what we want for our lives. There is a price to be paid, and that is to do the work. The good thing is that our work does not have to be laborious. Jesus said for us to come to Him because his "yoke is easy and his burdens are light." In other words, if we commit ourselves to doing what God says, then we have the opportunity to gain in every area of our lives. Napoleon Hill spells it out for us that when we are willing to do the work, then we can obtain the reward and also gain a rich, fulfilling life. The monetary wealth and riches will allow us to give free and change the world around us.

What needs to happen is that we must be determined to follow the path of wisdom, God's way of being and doing things. We have to be accountable for our actions. We become committed to the process of growth over time and also take time to renew our minds through the Word of God. Proverbs tells us that as a man or woman thinks, so is he or she. Our thoughts are where the battle is.

Prayer
Dear Lord, Help me to take advantage of all of the opportunities and blessings that you have for me. Help me to choose well and to follow Your ways of doing things. Bless me! Amen.

Word of the Day
Opportunities

Personal Meditations

Today's Prayer

38

Goodness: The Generous Person

Happy is the generous man, the one who feeds the poor.
—Proverbs 22:9 (TLB)

Lady Wisdom asks, "Who are you feeding?"

Generosity allows us to live a life of joy. When we are able to bless others, we are then blessing ourselves. It is less stressful to bless others than to curse them. Happiness becomes a part of our lifestyle, and it is not just based on ourselves but on living a life of sharing with others.

It is easy to give to others who can give back to us. However, when we are able to give to others who cannot bless us, then we are going deeper into the happy zone of God's love. We are taking on His characteristics of love. We become His hands and feet, bringing joy and peace, His kingdom to earth.

You may ask, "How can I give when I do not have much?" We were all given abilities and talents that, when used wisely, can produce resources that we can share with others. That ability will provide opportunities to advance. That is where happiness appears in our lives, when we are doing that special gift or talent and then sharing it with the most vulnerable. God will reward us when we bless others. One of His rewards is happiness, and happiness is priceless!

Prayer
Dear Lord, Thank You for the opportunity to give to the poor. I know it is not just giving them natural food to eat but also feeding people spiritual food that will improve their lives so they can draw close to You. Help me to be faithful in fulfilling this task. In Jesus's name, Amen.

Word of the Day
Generosity

Today's Prayer

39

Goodness: Pleasant as Perfume

Friendly suggestions are as pleasant as perfume.
—Proverbs 27:9 (TLB)

Lady Wisdom asks, "Are you generous with your words of wisdom?"

Generosity is not just giving people external things but also giving others internal blessings like a kind word. Words hold a lot of power and weight. There is value in a good quote or word of wisdom. Many of these words last the test of time. The living Bible is a good example of the power of the word. It says that the Word of God is powerful and sharper than any two-edged sword. It can get to the very root of any problem.

When we can provide friendly suggestions based on the revelatory Word of God, then we can enhance a person's life. Those words carry hope, which leads to success. We are then able to help someone find hope and healing. No one is beyond reach. It could be that one conversation filled with friendly suggestions can provide the solution to a life-threatening problem. Jesus can touch and reach anyone with love.

Some things we need to do when we are reaching out to hurting people are to be persistent with the kind words, authentic in giving them, encouraging, and innovative in presenting suggestions that are outside of the box. We are to add joy and humor to the conversation. Joy is a powerful medicine added with love and thoughtful words.

Prayer
Dear Lord, Help me to be mindful of the words I use when reaching out to a hurting person. I want the Holy Spirit to speak through me to the heart of the one whom You love. Amen.

Word of the Day
Mindfulness

Personal Meditations

Today's Prayer

40

Goodness: Work and Generosity

She sews for the poor, and generously gives to the needy.
—Proverbs 31:19–20 (TLB)

Lady Wisdom asks, "What does your work say about your generosity?"

The Proverbs 31 woman uses her work and worldly resources to benefit the poor. Her generosity becomes known around the community, and she is able to establish an atmosphere of caring for others. Others then follow her lead, and she is able to create an emotional garden of compassion.

Giving from the heart requires that the fruit of the Spirit has been cultivated and is growing. Being an agent of generosity requires that we must be willing to make sacrificial decisions. Our agenda becomes bigger than just trying to make money or a profit. To bring healing to the community involves giving of resources to meet a present need.

How to help someone find help and healing necessitates that we utilize our resources to provide tangible solutions. We have to think innovatively to change the present condition. It also may require a team of like-minded people to carry out the tasks. Persistence, creativity, cooperation, and time will make the work successful. In the end, we can become an agent for healing and positive change.

Prayer
Dear Lord, Help me not to get tired of doing good because Your Word says that in time we will have a harvest of blessing if we do not quit caring and imparting Your love to others. Amen.

Word of the Day
Blessings

Personal Meditations

Today's Prayer

41

Goodness: Needs Supplied!

If you give to the poor, your needs will be supplied! But
a curse upon those who close their eyes to poverty.
—Proverbs 28:27 (TLB)

Lady Wisdom asks, "Why do you not see the vulnerable person?"

There is a blessing in giving to the poor. "And I say unto you, Make to yourselves friends of the mammon of unrighteousness; that when ye fail, they may receive you into everlasting habitations (Luke 16:9, KJV)." The Bible tells us to use worldly wealth to make friends that when we are in need, others will give to us. Kindness and generosity provide an open door to blessings. The Lord Jesus went around doing acts of mercy and helping people who were experiencing poverty. He even went to the cross so we could be rich in all facets of our lives. To be Jesus followers, we too are expected to give to the poor. Giving has a way of multiplying itself.

On the other hand, a person who ignores the needs of the poor will find themselves poor in spirit and maybe poor in resources too. A person can be poor in spirit as well as poor in material things. I think that poverty in all of the areas of the human experience can cause a person to be stunted and not grow. There are deficiencies, a lack of motivation, and inadequate opportunities that can cause a person to fall into a poverty mind-set. However, with the seeing eyes of understanding and then with compassion, solutions can be discovered that can change the direction of a needy person.

Notable ways to meet the needs of others are giving to organizations that are already established who are meeting the physical needs of the poor and homeless. Volunteering time to a worthy cause and providing expert advice are ways of helping the poor. Starting a program or providing opportunities to learn new strategies of overcoming poverty can be a way of reaching people who may be overwhelmed by life's circumstances. The best thing to do is to ask God what He wants you to do and how you can help others. He will give insight and wisdom.

Prayer

Dear Lord, I want to make a difference in the lives of others who are experiencing poverty in my community. Please help me to find and do what You will have me to do to bring a solution to those who are hurting. Amen.

Word of the Day
Supplier

Today's Prayer

42

Goodness: Honor and Recognition

Praise her for the many find things she does. These
good deeds of hers shall bring her honor and
recognition from even the leaders of the nations.
—Proverbs 31:31 (TLB)

Lady Wisdom asks, "What are people saying about you? Do you have a good name?"

Having the right motives for doing good deeds will bring honor and recognition. People are moved when they see and hear of others helping the poor. We have many great examples of people who dedicated their lives to lifting up others.

I think our challenge is doing things that really matter. Give our time to worthy causes that have eternal rewards. Our commitments speak to our willingness to bring positive change. What we value the most is what we give our attention to. Doing things that carry hope and produce life are the "many fine things" that we can do.

How can we know what to do? First, we must consult God. He will give us a dream and assignment that is greater than ourselves. We will need His guidance to be able to create that great thing that He has ordained for us to do. We will also have to spend time listening to His voice and then gathering the resources needed to build the structure of compassion and innovation for others to thrive and be blessed. Honor comes from God. People will see God in us and reward our God-given efforts.

Prayer

Dear Lord, I want to do the things that matter and will bring You glory. Thank You, Lord, for giving me an assignment that will bless the world. Amen.

Word of the Day
Assignment

Personal Meditations

Today's Prayer

Planning and Developing

KINGDOM
BUILDING

43

Kingdom Building: How to Have a Satisfying Life

True humility and respect for the Lord lead a
man to riches, honor, and long life.
—Proverbs 22:4 (TLB)

Lady Wisdom asks, "Do you have the right priorities?"

There is a payoff for meekness (being humble) and fear of God. There is plenty of honor in a satisfying life. Laying your life down in total surrender to the Lord will bring a host of positive consequences that can make life very gratifying. It is like a natural response to doing life God's way.

God tells us in Deuteronomy 30:19 (KJV), "I call heaven and Earth to record this day against you, that I have set before you life and death, blessing and cursing: therefore choose life, that both thou and thy seed may live." Following His commandments will give us all we are looking for during our life journey.

Three things are promised: life, prosperity, and honor. These are all rewards for humbling ourselves before God and living life His way.

Prayer
Dear Lord, I am surrendering my life to You so I can have a satisfying life. Thank You for all of the benefits that come with submitting to You. Amen.

Word of the Day
Satisfying

Personal Meditations

Today's Prayer

44

Kingdom Building: Learn from the Ant

Take a lesson from the ants, you lazy fellow. Learn from their ways
and be wise. For though they have no king to make them work,
yet they labor hard all summer, gathering food for the winter.
—Proverbs 6:6–8 (TLB)

Lady Wisdom asks, "Are you tired of doing right, and will you miss
your harvest?"

I love what Galatians 6:9 (TLB) states, "And let us not get tired of doing
what is right, for, after a while, we will reap a harvest of blessing if we
don't get discouraged and give up." We can see this with the ant. It has
a determination to labor for the good of the ant community. The ant
realizes that if he does his work well now, he will later survive the winter.
The goal is to work for the common good of the ant nation.

There is something about doing our very best at tasks that we are
assigned and accomplishing the goals we have laid out for ourselves.
When we compete with ourselves and work on self-improvement, then
are we able to move closer to what God intended for us to be and to
do. We cannot ignore God and get away with it because God will
fulfill His creative plan for this world. The Bible says that the earth is
the Lord's ... and they that dwell within it. We must move in step to
His plans and His program. We will reap just the kind of crop we sow.
Living to please our own desires and not considering the greater good
of the community will lead to a harvest of spiritual decay, ending in
death. We want our lives to be planted with the wise things of the Spirit
so we will reap eternal life.

This idea of working together for a just cause will drive change in our society. We cannot get tired of wanting to build the kingdom of God in our communities. After a while, we will see the fruits of our labor. We must not get discouraged and quit. Being kind to everyone and helping each person to reach their potential will only lift the whole community. Everyone benefits because each person will be focused on walking the right path to success.

Prayer

Dear Lord, To build a thriving community, we need Your guidance and help in making wise and sound decisions that will benefit everyone. Help us to look to You as our source of knowledge, understanding, and wisdom. We want to discern the times well, knowing that we are working now in our summer so that when winter comes, we are prepared. Amen.

Word of the Day
Diligence

Today's Prayer

45

Kingdom Building: Wise Instructions Bring Wealth

My instruction is far more valuable than silver or gold. For the value
of wisdom is far above rubies; nothing can be compared with it.
—Proverbs 8:10–11 (TLB)

Lady Wisdom asks, "Why do you not receive instruction into the
hidden places of your heart so you can learn how to be wise?"

There are hidden places within us that block our ability to gain the
wisdom we need to move forward. These hidden places in our hearts
have been overtaken by squatters that are contaminating our thoughts.
Their work has been to stop the progress of God's plan for our lives.
Some of these squatters are fear, pride, arrogance, dishonesty, lack of
integrity, fear of the future, setbacks, stress, frustration, anxiety, worry,
depression, pressure, and seeking approval of others, to name a few.

Whenever Lady Wisdom speaks to us, these other voices contradict
what she is saying. Sometimes these voices sound like a trusted friend,
parent, or teacher. However, we must be able to develop the skill of
discerning the words of these squatters. The devil is the accuser of the
brethren. His role is to have these feelings come up, to prevent us from
trusting the words of Lady Wisdom.

It is necessary to be able to listen and know what is and is not wisdom.
King David in Psalms 51:6 (TPT) stated, "I know that you delight in
setting your truth deep in my spirit. So come into the hidden places
of my heart and teach me wisdom." Cleaning of the heart has to take
place. David used the following process:

1. King David admits his sins and asks the Lord to purify his conscience. He knows the love God has for him can override all of these voices and open up the channel of communication.
2. With a clean heart, David will be able to sing again. Singing has a way of changing the healing of the soul and restoring the emotions. The Word says that the joy of the Lord is our strength. With a clean heart, his joy will be able to give him the power to fight against the negative forces in attacking his heart.
3. Third, David asks for forgiveness. In the Lord's Prayer, Jesus teaches his disciples to ask for forgiveness and for them to forgive others too. It is by grace that we are saved. God's uncompromising love for us takes care of our sins through Jesus Christ.

Being filled with pure thoughts and holy desires must take up residence in our hearts. God has given us a new clean heart, and we want to make sure we do not find ourselves in the place of displeasing God. With a teachable spirit, we will find ourselves with a passion for life, and we will taste the joy of the Lord as the Holy Spirit holds us close. Our testimony will help others to recover from the hidden pain of the heart. We will have a road map that can show others how to find their way back home to God.

Prayer
Dear Lord, Help me to hide Your words deep in my heart so I will not do things that displease you. Amen.

Word of the Day
Instructions

Personal Meditations

Today's Prayer

46

Kingdom Building: Managing Your Days

I, Wisdom, will make the hours of your day more profitable
and the years of your life more fruitful ... Wisdom is its own
reward, and if you scorn her, you hurt only yourself.
—Proverbs 9:11—12 (TLB)

Lady Wisdom asks, "What is your obsession?"

Are you obsessed with what is happening in our society? What are you
focused on? Is this obsession providing you the spirit breath of life that
you need to enjoy your life? What we pay attention to dictates where we
are going. Our focus was given to us so we can complete assignments
and get things done. However, when we are distracted by things that do
not matter or are not truly important, we rob ourselves of the fullness
of joy spoken about in the Bible.

In God's presence, there is the fullness of joy. That is what we want to
spend the time meditating on, the Lord Jesus. This focus requires that
we forget about ourselves and look to the Holy Spirit to direct our minds
and thoughts to what really matters. I like what the Message Bible says
in Romans 8:5–8,

> Those who think they can do it on their own end up
> obsessed with measuring their own moral muscle but
> never get around to exercising it in real life. Those who
> trust God's action in them find that God's Spirit is in
> them—living and breathing God!

> Obsession with self in these matters is a dead end:
> attention to God leads us out into the open, into a

spacious, free life. Focusing on the self is the opposite of focusing on God. Anyone completely absorbed in self ignores God, ends up thinking more about self than God. That person ignores who God is and what he is doing. And God isn't pleased at being ignored.

Our mindset determines our life or death experience. To have our minds stayed on Jesus will bring us life and a flow that will bring others to the river in us. This joy the world cannot give, and the world cannot take it away. We can only lose it if we lose our focus and passion for God.

Prayer
Dear Lord, Thank You for revealing Yourself to us. Thank You, Lord, that we can have our minds and thoughts renewed so we can focus on You. You, Lord, are so incredible, and following You is so rewarding. So we ask that You will keep us obsessed with You and Your Word. Fix our hearts to receive all You have to offer so we can grow in the Holy Spirit and the life and peace that You give. Amen.

Word of the Day
Managing

Personal Meditations

Today's Prayer

47

Kingdom Building: While the Sun Shines

A wise youth makes hay while the sun shines, but what a
shame to see a lad who sleeps away his hour of opportunity.
—Proverbs 10:5 (TLB)

Lady Wisdom asks, "What is causing you to sleep? What has robbed
you of your energy?"

There are so many distractions in our society today. These distractions
can cause us to sleep and not be aware of the available opportunities.
We call these things "time robbers." Some of these time-wasters are
complaining, gossiping, watching TV, hanging out with negative
people, procrastinating, and doing unnecessary activities, to name a
few. The distractions can be a physical object or a mental diversion that
leaves one in a dream state or paralyzed for long periods. Not eating
right, not getting exercise, or not taking time to plan out the day leaves
us open to distractions that steal our ability to focus on what is most
important. Our life is experiencing a detour. We become tired and
overwhelmed. When we need to be alert and awake, we find ourselves
asleep, missing our hour of opportunity.

Finding out what our energy robbers are will then help us to regroup
and take back our willpower and strength. Those habits that allow us
to grow and become more excited about life will give us the energy to
focus on our dreams and goals. The practices that promote growth and
well-being must be incorporated into a daily routine. These actions will
help us to be prepared for our hour of opportunity.

There are things that we can do to make sure we are alert to what is
happening and following with God's will for our lives. Daily prayer and

biblical meditation will feed our minds and spirit. As we take time to commune with God, He reveals to us what we need to do next. Eating real food and drinking water will help to energize our body and give us the strength we need to finish tasks. Surrounding ourselves with like-minded people inspires us to look at opportunities and see the value in them. Having great mentors and counselors who can fill us with hope will provide a joyful expectation for good outcomes.

Spending time with God and His Word is the ultimate energizer. We are watering our souls and bringing light to our dreams. God's Word will give us the courage to get up and work because we know that with God, all things are possible.

Prayer
Dear Lord, I am grateful that You provide for us the hope we need to get up and work while the sun is shining and when opportunities abound. Help us not to get weary in doing the beneficial things that will propel our success. We need Your guidance and strength. Amen.

Word of the Day
Stay Alert

Personal Meditations

Today's Prayer

48

Kingdom Building: Good Influencers

The good influence of godly citizens causes a city to prosper;
but the moral decay of the wicked drives it downhill.
—Proverbs 11:11 (TLB)

Lady Wisdom asks, "Are you ready to be light in your city?"

Jesus commissioned His twelve disciples in the Bible to go out into the cities and towns and tell the good news of the gospel. His instructions were to preach this message, "Heaven's kingdom realm is accessible, close enough to touch." The way that they would bring the kingdom of heaven there is by healing the sick, disrupting the demonic presence, and bringing life back to the people. He told his disciples to free-release the healing power to others. They were not to use it for monetary gain. He said for them to "trust God for everything, because the one who works for him deserves to be provided for" (Matthew 10:5–10 TPT).

The Great Commission still holds weight in our time. Believers in Jesus Christ are to change the cities they live in and bring healing and prosperity to it. Without the active intervention of godly citizens in a city, the living conditions for those who are most vulnerable will deteriorate and decay. Greed and personal gain will overtake and bring harm to those who are not able to protect themselves from corrupt individuals. Godly citizens bring peace and prosperity to the city. People are able to thrive. Godly people care for the peace of God within them, changing the atmosphere and bringing heaven down to earth. The kingdom of heaven is where God resides. We are His ambassadors, extending His territory to each and every place where we speak His words and declare His gospel of the good news.

Bringing the kingdom of heaven to our cities can happen when other godly citizens come together to bring about change. With prayer, biblical meditation, and a listening ear to the Holy Spirit inside of us, we will be able to come up with transformable solutions to problems. Providing a climate of access and opportunity for all will change the mind-set of those who are overwhelmed with the issues of life. Speaking up with the message of hope and life will impact the direction of a city and therefore cause the city to prosper.

Prayer
Dear Lord, I thank You that You have imparted to us the authority to change the lives of people who are hurting and bring the kingdom of heaven to our cities and towns. Help us to go into our harvest fields with courage and grace. Give us the words to say so we can speak up with boldness and authority. Amen.

Word of the Day
Commissioned

Personal Meditations

Today's Prayer

49

Kingdom Building: Planning the Day's Agenda

She gets up before dawn to prepare breakfast for her
household and plans the day's work for her servant girls.
—Proverbs 31:15 (TLB)

Lady Wisdom asks, "What are you eating, or what is eating you?"

Jesus is the Bread of Life (John 6:22–59). He is the food we need for physical, emotional, and spiritual nourishment. The Bread of Life is the "supreme gift from God." When we focus on Jesus, then we are meditating on what He is saying, and we can learn His way of being and doing things. It is vital to move away from the idea that the world does things. Our man-made knowledge is so limiting. God is the one who created the world, so it makes sense to go to Him to find out what to do.

There is this gardener Paul Gautschi who began using wood chips to cover his land. He called his new discovery the "Back to Eden Method." He discovered the need to do this because he was located in an area where there was a limited supply of water. He asked God for help, and God gave him a new way of doing things. It's nature's style and the idea of the forest and woodlands. It is working so well that people visit his home each year to learn this new way, God's way of doing things.

We can gain new and innovative ways of doing things if we ask God for answers. It requires that we humble ourselves and listen to what He has to say. Listening is the key. Then we should write the vision down so we can run with it.

Prayer

Dear Lord, I thank You that You are filled with answers and that You want to help us through Holy Spirit and Lady Wisdom to be productive and successful in this life. I am looking to You to lead the way and provide the necessary knowledge, understanding, discernment, good judgment, common sense, and timing to do and complete all You have assigned for me to do in this world. Thank You for wisdom because I lack it in many areas. Bless me and my subscribers and listeners as we follow You and Your way. Amen.

Word of the Day
Innovation

Personal Meditations

Today's Prayer

50

Building Kingdom: Selling to the Merchants

She makes belted linen garments to sell to the merchants.
—Proverbs 31:24 (TLB)

Lady Wisdom asks, "Are you a producer or consumer?"

Building the kingdom of heaven is about creating an economy that can bring resources to a community so it can flourish. The Proverbs 31 woman knew that she needed to produce something that the merchants needed. She was a supplier of wholesale goods of belted linen garments. The merchants bought her products because they saw value in what she was providing for them. They had a market to sell her merchandise and make a profit.

Proverbs 18:15 TLB states, "The intelligent woman is always open to new ideas. In fact, she looks for them." I believe that this verse is true of the Proverbs 31 woman. She is innovative and creative. Thinking outside of the box helped her to see the possibilities of reaching a brand-new market of people. She was also willing to work with the merchants who could travel to these distant lands and sell her goods. She realized that she was part of an economic system of supply and demand. Since she was a woman open to new ideas, these ideas opened up a world of light and progress. She became a leader and a visionary in her community.

We too can be like the Proverbs 31 woman by asking the Creator to show us new ways of doing things. We can ask Him for wisdom and insight into the needs of our community and how we can become the supplier. There has to be a desire to want to see things in a new light. I also believe that our motives have to be right. How can we make things better? Biblical meditation and quiet time spent with God reveal the purpose of our lives, which is greater than our own personal gain. Beginning with God will expose us to a release of knowledge and creativity that will bring heaven to earth. God has the solutions, inventions, and creative insights that we need so we can prosper. We have to move from consumer to producer as we look to God for answers.

Prayer
Dear Lord, Help me to discover my life's meaning and purpose. I want to be a supplier of goods and products that meet the needs of everyone around me. I want to think outside the box and let my life be a testimony of Your greatness and glory. Amen.

Word of the Day
Discovery

Personal Meditations

Today's Prayer

51

Building Kingdom: Entrepreneur

She goes out to inspect a field and buys it; with
her own hands, she plants a vineyard.
—Proverbs 31:16 (TLB)

Lady Wisdom asks, "Are you in it for the long run?"

As entrepreneurs, we have a way of starting strong but midway becoming discouraged and deviating from the plan. However, Galatians 6:9 (KJV), "And let us not be weary in well doing: for in due season we shall reap, if we faint not." The Bible tells us not to let ourselves become weary or disheartened in planting good seeds, for in the right season of reaping we will gather a wonderful harvest. The harvest will come. Sometimes it is easier said than believed, especially when what we have been doing has taken years to come to pass.

I love the fact that the Proverbs 31 woman is thinking long term. She takes the time to inspect the field. She looks to see how much value she can produce from this investment. She wants to verify the conditions of the field and note anything that may hinder her from having a productive field of crops. She wants to know if there are any shortcomings; therefore she looks into these details before purchasing the land.

After the inspection, the Proverbs 31 woman has determined that the field is worth purchasing, and she goes ahead and buys it. She does not stop there but gets busy working the land. At the beginning of any venture, it is necessary to have some understanding of how the business works. It is up to the business owner to take the time to plan, implement, and create. Dedication is required to get the business off the ground. She lays a solid foundation with a strong plan as she begins working on transforming the field.

Starting a business can be easy to do, especially if you have an idea that solves a problem or meets a need. Taking time to determine your strengths and passions will help to build the confidence needed to start the business. Asking God for wisdom to make the right decisions along the way will help you to avoid unnecessary problems. Knowing that God is guiding you will empower you to continue to work your field. You have the advantage because you have the guidance of the Lord.

Prayer
Dear Lord, Help me listen to Your voice so I can buy the right field and get busy making it productive. Amen.

Word of the Day
Inspection

Personal Meditations

Today's Prayer

Refining with the Tool of

PRAYER

52

Prayer: Moving to the Beat of God's Heart!

My son, never forget the things I've taught you. If you want
a long and satisfying life, closely follow my instructions.
Never forget to be truthful and kind. Hold these virtues
tightly. Write them deep within your heart.
—Proverbs 3:1–3 (TLB)

Lady Wisdom asks, "What is taking the place of God's Word in your heart?"

Timing is everything! Have you ever been to a church service in which the drummer could not keep a beat? In that moment, it made it difficult to flow with the music because the beat was not right. However, experiencing a great drummer playing and keeping the timing just makes you want to dance and sing. There is joy in moving to the sound and flow from the beat of the drum.

There is rhythm in the garden, and when we move to the beat of the garden, then are we able to produce. A beat can be found in the land. The garden has its own pulse or rhythm. When we find it, then are we able to get things done. The plot produces for us. We are moving together in harmony. Asking the garden to produce out of rhythm is very frustrating, and what will happen is that insects and other things in the ground will come and cut it down. Nature works together to grow, prune, and compost. With the appropriate movement in the allotment, you will see productivity and a harvest.

If we are a garden, then there is a rhythm to our lives. Our heartbeat gives us the tempo. Also our daily devotion with God informs us how to move through life with the right timing. When we find the beat of God's heart, don't let it go!

Prayer
Dear Lord, I want to move according to Your heartbeat. Help me to be diligent in all I do. I want to let my heartbeat be the same as heavenly Father. That way, I know I am moving with Him and His will for my life. It just makes everything so much easier and more enjoyable. I want to be carried by His strength and flow in the river of His love. Amen.

Word of the Day
Timing

53

Prayer: Strength and Courage

Cling to wisdom—she will protect you.
Love her—she will guard you.
—Proverbs 4:6 (TLB)

Lady Wisdom asks, "Are you allowing your love for wisdom strengthen you?"

Strength and courage for this day seem to be the theme. At the beginning of the month, at the beginning of anything, I need power and courage. Many questions fill my mind: what if I am wasting my time? Will this work? What do I need to focus on? What is the most important? These questions all have some validity to them. Yet I know that I must begin and move forward in faith for the next victory. Nothing will be accomplished if I do nothing.

The verse for the day in the Bible app I refer to almost every day is Deuteronomy 31:6 (KJV), "Be strong and of a good courage, fear not, nor be afraid of them: for the Lord thy God, he it is that doth go with thee; he will not fail thee, nor forsake thee." This is the promise that the Lord also gives to us. Be strong! Be courageous! Fear not! Do not be afraid! I, God, am with you! Isn't this fantastic that God is our encourager and that He knows just what we need to know?

Prayer
Dear Lord, I want to have all of the faith I need to move forward. I want to fulfill the plans You have for me. I can rest in the truth of Your Word. What You said, You will do! I know You will give me strength and provide me with courage as I lean on and believe Your Word. I will take action! Amen.

Word of the Day
Faith

Personal Meditations

Today's Prayer

54

Prayer: God, Give Me Peace in My Heart!

For the Lord grants wisdom! His every word is a
treasure of knowledge and understanding.
—Proverbs 2:6 (TLB)

Never forget to be truthful and kind. Hold these virtues tightly. Write
them deep within your heart.

—Proverbs 3:3 (TLB)

Lady Wisdom asks, "Have you stored every word of wisdom given to
you in your heart?"

Many people are walking around with pain in their hearts. To be able
to encourage the spirit of peace in our environment first, we have to
get our heart right with God. You may say that you are born again and
that Jesus lives in your heart. I believe that is true. There things need
to move out so the Holy Spirit can take up every corner of your private
house. We want to be a home for God's Holy Spirit.

What is inside that makes you so anxious or uncomfortable? Who do
you dread seeing or being around? Why do you feel anger or pain in
some places? Questions like these will help us to examine our thoughts,
emotions, and deeply hidden feelings. "Beloved, I wish above all things
that thou mayest prosper and be in health, even as thy soul prospereth
(3 John 1:2, KJV)." The Bible says that we can prosper and be in health
even as our souls prosper. Our soul is made up of our mind, will, and
emotions.

Do you have joy in your heart? Does peace reside there? I believe that
the spirit of joy and peace has been given to us to help us overcome

life's tests and trials. We can have these raging thoughts of murmuring, complaining, and discord removed. Jesus gave us His peace when He was leaving the earth. He said, "My peace, I leave with you." We can offer a prayer of peace to be our companion and help us remove other forces that are not from Jesus. Jesus is our Prince of Peace.

Prayer
Dear Lord, I know that prayer is the tool I need to use to help me move closer to God. You want me to spread peace to others. Help me to make sure that the Holy Spirit's wisdom, joy, and peace fills my heart. Amen.

Word of the Day
Spread and Fill

Personal Meditations

Today's Prayer

55

Prayer: Heal the Hidden Pain in my Soul

The good man's life is full of light. The
sinner's road is dark and gloomy.
—Proverbs 13:9 (TLB)

Lady Wisdom asks, "Are you resting in the healing words of God?"

First, I want to thank You, heavenly Father, for loving me. You care about me to make me aware that there are hidden hurts in my soul that need to be healed. I am grateful for this revelation. God, my soul needs to be restored and healed from past hurts and trauma I do not remember but are blocking my progress in You. Please let me rest in the meadow grass of Your kindness and lead me beside the quiet streams of Your love. You can restore my failing health and help me do what honors You the most.

Old hurts and pains—as well as the hidden things that have happened in my life that are keeping me back from joy—please bring them to the surface so I can deal with them and let you heal me. I want to be whole in You. I want to experience all of the goodness You have for me in this life. I want to become the fullest expression of whom You want me to be.

Just like a stressed plant that cannot resist the bugs and diseases that attack it, I feel sometimes the vulnerability of my past that wants to block my future. Please help me to confront those areas of my life that remain dark and covered up by things.

I realize that I cannot do this work by myself, so I am asking for the aid of the Holy Spirit to guide me through this process. The Comforter is kind and will not hurt me. But He will refresh my soul. So therefore I say "Yes!" to this work.

Prayer
Dear Lord, I am looking for freedom, peace, and joy to replace any pain or hurt and to heal the wounds of life, making me completely whole in You, my Lord. Thank You for this day and the beginning of this healing process. Amen.

Word of the Day
Healing

Personal Meditations

Today's Prayer

56

Prayer: Attitude of Thanksgiving

True humility and respect for the Lord lead a
man to riches, honor and long life.
—Proverbs 22:4 (TLB)

Lady Wisdom asks, "How are you honoring God?"

There is a level of humility needed to be able to receive blessings. Refusing a gift given based on its appearance can be a sign that the person has a proud spirit. The value placed on the gift is measured by the humility and respect we have for the giver. If we truly honor the gift and the giver of the gift, then we will receive it with humility and reverence. The feeling of thankfulness will be the dominant posture for receiving the gift.

Just like when we say "thank you" to the person who gives us a gift, so it is when we say "thank You" to God. The person giving the gift is satisfied that we recognize their generosity to us. There is that release of happiness and contentment. The person loves to give more presents because they know you will welcome and value the effort and time taken to create the gift for you.

When we pray and give thanks to God, He is satisfied with our understanding of His kindness and mercy to us. God has been so good to us, and He has blessed us each day. As we release the praises to God, He receives the glory. We become more aware of His goodness and then share it with others. God's joy in us becomes contagious, and others are infected with this abundant thankfulness. It spreads.

Prayer

Dear Lord, I pray that we will have an attitude of thanksgiving and adoration. Let us pray and praise God for everything. May we be filled with thanksgiving and worship to God for His goodness and mercy to us as we go through our day. Amen.

Word of the Day
Adoration

Personal Meditations

Today's Prayer

57

Prayer: Praying Spirit-led Prayers

It is the glory of God to conceal a thing: but the
honour of kings is to search out a matter.
—Proverbs 25:2 (KJV)

Lady Wisdom asks, "Do you ever feel unfulfilled in prayer?"

Have you prayed about a matter but did not have any peace after praying? There is a much more productive way of praying, and that is to pray God's prayer. The scriptures in the Bible can be used to pray what God says. Finding the verses that speak to our concerns and then praying them will release the peace we are looking for.

These prayers become spirit-led prayers. Being led by the Holy Spirit can bring peace in your heart and satisfaction. It will create a sense of it as a done deal. Holy Spirit prayers do not need to be long. It can be a paragraph, a sentence, a word, or a grain. The result we want is that we know that God has heard us and that we believe that He will meet the need and answer the prayer.

Spirit-led prayers are oftentimes short and to the point. There is that sense of satisfaction, and it is already completed. These prayers tend to be eternal. God wants to bless us and see us grow and develop in Him. He will lead us into a deeper relationship with Him as we seek out His will for our lives. We just need to daily commit our will and actions to fulfilling His will, and then we will see our prayers answered.

Prayer
Dear Lord, I am asking for things that are more lasting and may need to be developed in me. The fruit of the Spirit is what I need to increase

in my life. Holy Spirit, I know You are interested in growing in me. Please reveal my motives. I want a deeper relationship with God. How can I be a better person today? Amen.

Word of the Day
Lasting

58

Prayer: Cultivate Your Gifts

We should make plans—counting on God to direct us.
—Proverbs 16:9 (TLB)

Lady Wisdom asks, "Is God in your plans?"

Within your heart, we can make plans for our future, but the Lord chooses the steps we take to get there. At times, I feel I am in control of my life, but only to be reminded that it is God who makes it look so easy. When I do not consult God, I find that whatever I want to do is more difficult and becomes a burden. Listening and doing is the key to great success in life—doing life God's way. So this is my prayer for this day.

Prayer
Dear Lord, Help me to appreciate the gifts and talents that You have given me and cultivate them. First, give me clear vision of what the talents and gifts are that you have endowed me with. I want to be able to recognize what talents and giftings that I have. Second, help me to hear Your voice speaking to me through these abilities and gifts so I can master my abilities and gifts with skill and grace. Third, lead me each step of the way to discover why You have gifted me this way and to follow the pathway and steps that You have ordained for me to go. Thank You for blessing my small steps and helping me to focus on what You have gifted me to do. I want to excel for Your honor and glory and to bless, assist, and support others on their journey in life. Help me to do what I am good at and not quit! Amen.

Word of the Day
Cultivate

59

Prayer: Thank You, Lord, for Hope

My son, honey whets the appetite, and so does wisdom! When you
enjoy becoming wise, there is hope for you! A bright future lies ahead!
—Proverbs 24:13–14 (TLB)

Lady Wisdom asks, "Whose career is it: yours or God's?"

I am thankful for God's definition of hope. God's hope leads to the
fulfillment of the promise. It says that hope does not make us ashamed.
We can hope with confidence. God is a covenant-keeping God. He is
not like us; He does not breaks His promises. His Word is precious, so
He honors His Word. Therefore when we receive revelation-knowledge
about what God has for us, we can go forward with assurance that it
will come to pass if we have the faith to believe.

Building our hope is a process. We have to remind ourselves of God's
goodness. What has God done for you in the past? If He did it before,
then He can do it again. Have faith in God. Therefore, hope is a joyful
expectation for great things to come. Hope leads to breakthroughs in
our life.

God is saying to us to go ahead, build your career, and give yourself
to your work. But if you put Him first, you'll see your family built up.
The success we are looking for is not just for ourselves but will provide
the hope needed for the future. Our hope in the Lord will carry on for
generations to come.

Prayer
Dear Lord, Help me to cultivate hope. I choose to believe You and what You have promised me. Bless my career, family, and the generations to come. Amen.

Word of the Day
Hope

Personal Meditations

Today's Prayer

60

Prayer: Great Expectation

Hope deferred makes the heart sick, but a
longing fulfilled is a tree of life.
—Proverbs 13:12 (KJV)

Lady Wisdom asks, "Why are you letting go of your hope?"

Prayer
Dear Lord, I honor You. I am grateful that You are in my life. I want
to thank You that You have allowed me to have a relationship with You
through Jesus Christ our Lord. I do not have to figure things out by
myself, but I can call on the wisdom of heaven to help guide me through
my day. I want You to know that I do not take this for granted because
I know that if I listen and obey Your loving instructions, then I will
reap so much joy and peace.

You are my great expectation. I am praying in faith, trusting and
believing You to give me the best advice and leading me into my place
of comfort and satisfaction. Lord, I want to end this day satisfied with
everything I do, knowing I have fulfilled the tasks assigned for this
day. I expect that You will demonstrate your supernatural power in
everything I do and You will add your super to my natural.

Help me walk in faith and confidence in who You are and what You
can do. Help me not to doubt Your Word or let fear get the best of me.
Help me not to delay on completing the things that You have assigned
me to do but instead be diligent and persistent in following through
with each task. Bless my readers, subscribers, followers, and listeners.

I declare that our hearts trust completely in God. We know that God will come through for us. We are certain and confident in His love for us. Our hopes and expectations are from God. Thank You, Lord, for answering our prayers and giving us what we need to obey Your instructions for this day. Amen.

Word of the Day
Grateful

Personal Meditations

Today's Prayer

61

Prayer: Giving Grace

Don't be conceited, sure of your own wisdom. Instead, trust
and reverence the Lord, and turn your back on evil; when you
do that, then you will be given renewed health and vitality.
—Proverbs 3:7–8 (TLB)

Lady Wisdom asks, "Why don't you give some grace to yourself and give more grace to others?"

Lord, I need to be more patient with the people who are close to me and to be their cheerleader during difficult times. I need also, Lord, to be more patient with myself and allow time for learning and growing.

Help me, Lord, to do better! Lord, I know You are changing me into a better person and transforming me into Your image. I know I have a long way to go, but help me to be patient with myself and enjoy my life each day.

Help me to extend that grace to others and to look a little more deeply at their situation, giving them the benefit of the doubt before judging them and their motives. When others snub me or make me feel bad, help me to remember that they are in the process of becoming too.

I pray that we will remember that we are being renewed day by day. So we are not giving up. Even though on the outside it often looks like things are falling apart, on the inside where You are, You are helping us to experience new life full of joy and creativity, especially in the garden. Thank You for not letting a day go by without Your unfolding grace. The things in our lives are here today but will be gone tomorrow. But what You are developing in us will last forever, like Your love, joy, and peace, and it will increase grace.

Prayer
Dear Lord, Help me to realize that we all have our insecurities and are trying to figure out life too. Help me to give others a little grace and tolerance. Help me to be patient with myself and compassionate toward others today. Amen.

Word of the Day
Grace

Today's Prayer

62

Prayer: Are You Mad at God?

A man is a fool to trust himself! But those
who use God's wisdom are safe.
—Proverbs 28:26 (TLB)

Lady Wisdom asks, "Why are you letting things block your relationship with God?"

Do not be bitter with God! He is your friend that sticks closer than your own brother. Your bitterness will hinder your ability to hear from God. Refuse to become bitter, but instead lean in closer to God because there is something He wants to tell you and the devil does not want you to hear. Ephesians 4:31 (KJV) states, "Lay aside bitter words temper tantrums revenge profanity and insults."

Prayer
Dear Lord, Help me to let You fight my battles. I want to stay humble before You. I want to trust You. Amen.

Word of the Day
Lean In

Personal Meditations

Today's Prayer

63

Prayer: Praising My Way to His Presence

Wisdom is the tree of life to those who eat her fruit;
happy is the man who keeps on eating it.
—Proverbs 3:18 (TLB)

Lady Wisdom asks, "Why are you overwhelmed and discouraged?"

I declare, "When my heart is overwhelmed, I will praise my way into Your presence."

Prayer
Dear Lord, We praise and worship You this day. We want to begin our day with You. We anticipate many blessings coming our way, so we want You to remove everything that will block the movement of Your hand in our lives. We desire Your presence, so we worship and praise You.

Lord, I make myself available to You to hear your voice. I enter into Your presence, humbly respecting who You are and what You have done. With abundant praise, I lift my heart to You and ask You to fill me to full capacity with Your love, joy, and peace.

I genuinely praise You and worship You from a childlike heart because You are my heavenly Father and I know You love me. So I come boldly into Your presence, knowing You have great things in store for me this day. Help me to be mindful of all of Your blessings, the small things as well as the enormous, spectacular things. All of Your benefits are "Yes!" and "Amen!" in my life.

I know I will prosper even as my soul prospers. So shine Your great light in every corner of my heart and mind, and I want the Holy Spirit to guide me in the cleanup of every hidden sin or event that has blocked my progress with You.

Bless me today. Open up doors and windows, and let Your fresh air come into my life and the atmosphere around me. Thank You for answering my prayers. Amen.

Word of the Day
Praising

Today's Prayer

64

Prayer: Working from My Full Capacity

I, Wisdom, give good advice and common sense.
Because of my strength, kings reign in power.
—Proverbs 8:14–15

Lady Wisdom asks, "Why are you not working from your full capacity?"

Have you ever wondered why you seem to fall short of getting the full benefits of a situation? It could be that we are not working from our full capacity. There is that inside information that is missing, which can revolutionize our way of doing things. What we need is God's wisdom to expand our understanding and give us the applied know-how on how to get the results that we are looking for. Jesus has promised that He will ask the Father, and God will give you another advocate, the Holy Spirit, to help you and be with you forever.

God's wisdom is more complete and comprehensive. He tells us in the book of James 1:5 (KJV), "If any of you lack wisdom, let him ask of God, that giveth to all men liberally and upbraidth not, and it shall be given him." If we want insight to a situation, ask Him. All we are required to do is to believe. Having confidence in God involves getting to know how He thinks about a matter.

We have to ask Him and then listen. Follow up with the completion of the task. Obedience is key to progressing with the Holy Spirit. It is a step-by-step process of assignments that lead to a prosperous end. Many begin walking with God, but those who finish the process win.

Therefore, each day it is important to take time to get the instructions for the day. First, we have to humble ourselves and pray. Seek His guidance for the day. We must listen and take notes. He says for us to write the vision down so we can run with it. Biblical meditation is so vital to the success of the dream.

We want to function from our full capacity. Recognize the resources that are available to us so we can experience the true success that God will provide. Lady Wisdom tells me in Proverbs that wealth, position, and power received the wrong way leads to death. So we need the Holy Spirit to show us the way. We want to draw on His ability. Then we can accomplish more.

Prayer
Dear Lord, Thank You for giving me the Comforter, the Holy Spirit, that he will remain with me forever. Amen.

Word of the Day
Full Capacity

Personal Meditations

Today's Prayer

65

Prayer: God Speaks in Different Ways

In everything you do, put God first, and he will
direct you and crown your efforts with success.
—Proverbs 3:6 (TLB)

Lady Wisdom asks, "Listen! Do you want success?"

We must listen for God's voice in everything we do and everywhere
we go. God is the one who will keep us on track. God is speaking!
Are you listening? God speaks to us about what is right and good for
us. He is dependable. He speaks to us in many ways, like through
His Word, nature, people, circumstances, peace, wisdom, supernatural
intervention dreams, visions, and what some call the inner witness or
a knowing.

He also speaks to us in a still, small voice or the inner witness. We just
know it is not ourselves talking and we need to listen. God is calling us
to do a task or assignment or to fulfill a goal or purpose. The question
is: Are we listening?

Prayer
Dear Lord, We want to hear Your voice; however, You want to speak to
us. I know You love us. You have good plans for us. Help us to listen
and then obey your voice because it is only for our good. Amen.

Word of the Day
Dependable

Personal Meditations

Today's Prayer

66

Prayer: Willpower or Holy Spirit Power?

But the good man walks along in the ever-brightening light
of God's favor; the dawn gives way to morning splendor,
while the evil man gropes and stumbles in the darkness.
—Proverbs 4:18–19 (TLB)

Lady Wisdom asks, "Holy Spirit's power or your power, which is it?"

Prayer
Dear Lord, I thank You that Your Holy Spirit is present to help us live a life that is pleasing to You. We want to enjoy the life You have destined for us to have. I try to run my life, but I find that my mind, will, and emotions always lead me to a stuck place. I end up doing the things I don't want to do. My willpower becomes weak, and I succumb to what my emotions want me to do.

Lord, I am tired of falling prey to my emotions and fears. I am asking You for Holy Spirit assistance in increasing my resistance to the things that make me fall short of Your glory. I want to be Spirit-led. My willpower and discipline are needed and essential to having a productive life. But I realize that is not enough to be able to live a wisdom/God-centered life. I want to make it across the finish line and accomplish my purpose for being here.

So dear heavenly Father, I am asking for my subscribers and me that You release Your power into my willpower and that you energize us so we can fulfill Your purpose for us and we can finish our assignments strong. We will give You all of the glory and praise because we know that without Your holy power, we could not get the job done.

I want to walk and live habitually in the Holy Spirit. I want to be responsive to and controlled and guided by your spirit of love. I know I will certainly not gratify the cravings and desires of the flesh of my human nature without God when I am living in the presence of grace and truth.

Thank You in advance for leading the way and giving us the power to achieve success today. In Jesus' mighty name, Amen.

Word of the Day
Willpower

Personal Meditations

Today's Prayer

67

Prayer: Take Time to Laugh

Deceit fills hearts that are plotting for evil; joy
fills hearts that are planning for good!
—Proverbs 12:20 TLB

Lady Wisdom asks, "Are you taking time to laugh?"

Prayer
Dear Lord, I am happy that You are a God of joy! You tell us to be satisfied and not to worry. Yet we find ourselves oftentimes worrying about what will happen next when we do not have control over our future. We can plan for the future, but ultimately You direct our steps. We are grateful that You want to be actively involved in our lives. However, You will not make us do anything that we do not want to do. You, my Lord, are not a bully.

Help me and my subscribers and listeners to not be anxious and worried because of the many dangerous things happening in the world. Yes, we need to acknowledge them and be prepared. However, help us to relax and take things as they come. Help us not to get upset but to sit back and ask You, "What does this all mean?"

Thank You for giving us opportunities to laugh and sing for joy. When we wake up in the morning, help us to look for comfort in the day. You want us to enjoy every moment of our lives. Thank You, Lord, that life with You is not boring. Each day is filled with new mercies, a new adventure, and new experiences that can make us excited about living and sharing our lives with others.

Lord, help me not to get upset but to laugh and not expect perfection from myself all of the time. Help me to let myself grow in You and grow through prayer as I enjoy my life this day. Therefore, I will be glad in the Lord and rejoice. I will be uncompromisingly righteous about it. I will be upright and in right standing with God. I will shout for joy as I desire to be upright in heart! Celebrate God. Sing together, everyone!

I will have an honest heart and raise the roof while I rejoice in the Lord and am glad. I will obey Him and shout for joy. My heart is pure toward God. Thank You, Jesus! Amen.

Word of the Day
Laugh

Today's Prayer

68

Prayer: Lord, Transform My Life!

> I want those already wise to become the wiser and become leaders
> by exploring the depths of meaning in these nuggets of truth.
> —Proverbs 1:5–6 (TLB)

Lady Wisdom asks, "Do you need a life transformation?"

Our correct response to God's marvelous mercies should be a life transformed by love. I encourage you to surrender yourselves to God to be his sacred, living sacrifice as the Bible tells us. We do this by living in holiness, experiencing all that delights God's heart. The Word of God says that this becomes our genuine expression of worship. Therefore, we surrender our lives to God in worship.

Prayer
Dear Lord, I want to stop imitating the ideals and opinions of the culture around me. I want to be transformed by the Holy Spirit inwardly. Help me to be willing to transform my thinking and think Your thoughts. Please give me a total overhaul of how I feel about things and do them.

Father, we want to discern Your will for our lives. We also want to live a beautiful life. We want an experience that is satisfying and perfect in your eyes. So I also pray this prayer for my readers, subscribers, and listeners. I pray that they too may experience the joy of the Lord and the peace You offer.

I pray for my readers, subscribers, and listeners that You will empower them with the knowledge of who You are and why You want to improve their lives through Your love. And last, I pray for my readers, subscribers, and listeners that You will fill them with the desire to apply Your knowledge to their everyday experiences. Help them to surrender their days in worship to You, even as the garden and nature worship You.

Thank You for answering our prayers and giving us a day of worship and gratitude for all You have done and will do as we listen and follow You. In Jesus's name we pray. Amen.

Word of the Day
Transform

69

Prayer: Words Are Containers of Power!

> Self-control means controlling the tongue! A
> quick retort can ruin everything.
> —Proverbs 13:3 (TLB)

Lady Wisdom asks, "Are your words filled with complaining and grumbling, or are they filled with joy and peace?"

"Death and life are in the power of the tongue: and they that love it shall eat the fruit thereof (Proverbs 18:21 KJV)." It tells us the power of the tongue can bring life or death. Words are containers of power. What we say can bless us or hurt us. Words spoken over a community can set the tone for destruction or inspire godly change. Complaining opens many doors to the enemy. It is a corrupt type of conversation that creates many problems. This destructive form of communication does affect the people who have to listen to it. Foul, polluting words bring curses and every evil. When we complain about our present circumstances, we remain in it. It contaminates the future and can lead to death.

Prayer
Dear Lord, I want to ask for forgiveness for complaining and grumbling. God, You tell us to speak life into our situations. I want to praise You amidst difficulty. That is how You, God, get the glory, and He is faithful to raise us out of the mess. The right way to start my day is with gratitude and thanksgiving to God. Praise is a weapon that unlocks the spirit of hope. Filling my thoughts with the goodness of God and declaring it sets the tone and cleanses the atmosphere for great things to happen. I want to be one of the people who are busy giving You, God, praise and thanks to be a grateful person and not complain.

I want to give You praise and thanksgiving every day because I know You will strengthen me and help me to bring Your kingdom to our families, community, and this world. "Thy kingdom come. Thy will be done!" Amen.

Word of the Day
Speak Life!

Personal Meditations

Today's Prayer

70

Prayer: Enjoy Your Excellent Life with God

For whoever finds me (Lady Wisdom) finds
life and wins approval from the Lord.
—Proverbs 8:35 (TLB)

Lady Wisdom asks, "What kind of life do you have without God? Is it excellent?"

In planting a garden, laws and standards must be followed for success. God is so faithful to us and wants us to grow and flourish that He also gave us Lady Wisdom and the Proverbs 31 woman to show us how to live. He gave us the book of Proverbs, the manual for living, so we can make good and wise decisions that will bring life and prosperity to everyone in our community. We also have an ideal or exemplar in which we measure our progress. Let us make sure that Jesus is our standard for success. Father God provided Him as an example of how we should live our lives.

We can have an excellent life with God, if we are willing to take the time to follow His instructions by listening to and reading His Word. We also must be doers of His Word through writing the vision and speaking the truth of the kingdom of heaven.

My prayer is that we find the ways of God so exciting and rewarding that we can't turn back to the old ways of doing things. We want to go God's way. I also pray that we realize that God has given us all we need to live a life that is pleasing to Him. We can find joy in planting, cultivating, and harvesting the dreams and blessings of the garden of our lives.

Prayer

Dear Lord, Thank You for all You have done for us. We come to you with a heart of gratitude and thanksgiving for opening up our understanding to the blessings of wisdom. Your way gives us a satisfying life, and we can experience excellence and joy because of Your love. Therefore, we are filled with joy and peace. Thank You! Amen.

Word of the Day
Excellent Life

Personal Meditations

Today's Prayer

Strengthening with the Tool of

PRAISE

71

Praise: The First Step

How does a man become wise? The first step is to trust and
reverence the Lord! Only fools refuse to be taught. Listen
to your father and mother. What you learn from them will
stand you in good stead; it will gain you many honors.
—Proverbs 1:7–9 (TLB)

Lady Wisdom asks, "Are you thankful for your parents?"

Wisdom is all around us. We can see wisdom working in nature.
However in relationships, we are given the opportunity to be educated
in wisdom from our parents. One of the Ten Commandments tells us
to honor our father and mother. "Honor your father and your mother
that you may live long, good life in the land the Lord your God will
give you" (Exodus 20:12 TLB).

Honoring our parents is also how we honor the Almighty by giving
them respect. In the New Testament, we are also reminded to honor
our father and mother because it comes with a promise. Honor is respect
and esteem to the people who birthed you. Your parents are not perfect
so that respect is not given to them because of their perfection but rather
the role or position in which God has placed them in your life. They
were the life force that came together to give birth to you. Therefore
they deserve your respect and honor.

We can all learn from our parents. We can learn what to do and what
not to do by observing their life. If your parents are believers in Jesus
Christ, then their wisdom is hopefully based on the Word of God.
Still, there is wisdom given by experience. There are things that your
parents encountered that taught them lessons for living. These lessons

concerning relationships, family, finance, and work, to name a few, can provide knowledge and insight into navigating the world.

How does a person become wise? I believe by first respecting the gift of our parents and then learning from their lives. Remember their words of wisdom and apply what we have been taught to issues that are presented to us. We must trust and revere God by celebrating and giving thanks for our earthly parents. Thank You, God!

Prayer
Dear Lord, Thank You for my parents. I am grateful that they decided to birth me into the world. I am also grateful for godly parents who taught me to love you. Amen.

Word of the Day
First Step

Personal Meditations

Today's Prayer

72

Praise: Words to Heart

But all who listen to me shall live in peace and safety, unafraid.
—Proverbs 1:33 (TLB)

Lady Wisdom asks, "Are you taking my words to heart?"

I remember when I was experiencing a difficult time in my spiritual life. I had felt rejection from the people whom I thought wanted me. It was a very lonely and disappointing time. A friend of mine gave me a scripture in Psalms 37:3 (NLT) that stated a similar word, "Trust in the LORD and do good. Then you will live safely in the land and prosper."

Another version stated that I needed to cultivate faithfulness. I had never focused on the word *faithfulness* before, so when I say it, I knew that was what I needed to do. Teaching children was my career goal, and then leading a school became my dream. So I decided to cultivate this work and follow my career path with fidelity. Psalm 37 became my road map.

I believe that God is faithful to us and He knows what will bring out the best in us. Sometimes we do not understand, but He has a plan for our lives. When we listen to the Lord, then we are able to find the answers we are looking for. Each experience we have in which we follow the path of love and peace, the greater we become confident in hearing God's voice. His ways become higher and better than ours.

I am thankful that God's Word is true. There is a place of peace and safety in Him. When we find that place through biblical meditation and prayer, we are able to rest in Him with a heart of joy. The natural response to the joy is praise. The Bible tells us that the joy of the Lord is our strength. So therefore we are able to rejoice and sing for joy.

Prayer
Dear Lord, Thank You for the confidence we have in Your Word. Help us be attentive to Your voice and listen. Thank You for the strength to follow through and do what You say. Amen.

Word of the Day
God's Heart

Today's Prayer

73

Praise: Young Man, Listen

Every young man who listens to me and obeys my
instructions will be given wisdom and good sense.
—Proverbs 2:1 (TLB)

Lady Wisdom asks, "Are you thankful for good instruction, wisdom, and good sense?"

Having a listening ear to what Lady Wisdom has to say is vital to our success. Taking in instructions requires we find a quiet place free from distractions. Praying first with a heart of thanksgiving and expectance will release the willingness to hear what God has to say. Then ask the Lord what His will is for our life. Getting the instructions directly from God means He is obligated to anoint what He wants to see accomplished.

It is our responsibility to obey His commands. We are to meditate on His Word, day and night. A sustained focus on what God is saying will open up to us the details of what needs to be done. I find that I long for God's help and assistance. I discover myself questioning Him, wanting to find out if I am doing things His way. The lines of communication stay open. This allows me to seek His counsel and apply godly wisdom.

I find that early in the morning around 5:00 a.m. when the house is quiet is the best time to listen to the voice of God inside. There have not been any distractions, and I am able to concentrate on what the assignment is for the day or the season in my life. I think daily prayer and meditation helps to clarify things that may seem confusing. Our walk with God means following His step-by-step instructions.

Prayer
Dear Lord, Thank You for taking the time to give me instructions. I want step-by-step instructions from You. Help me to listen and obey so You will continue leading me on the path to success. Amen.

Word of the Day
Take Time

Personal Meditations

Today's Prayer

74

Praise: Treasure of Knowledge and Understanding

For the Lord grants wisdom! His every word is a
treasure of knowledge and understanding.
—Proverbs 2:6 (TLB)

Lady Wisdom asks, "Are you thankful for the treasure of knowledge and understanding?"

I am thankful that the Lord grants me wisdom. Proverbs 2:4–6 tells us that if we seek His wisdom like we seek silver and search for his applied heavenly knowledge like treasure that is buried, then we begin to understand the reverent and worshipful fear of the Lord. God gives us the applied knowledge that we are looking for. He will speak to us.

I am thankful for the treasure of knowledge and understanding! The treasure can be found. We must have the desire to want to look for it. If we obey God in every little thing, then we can enjoy our lives to the fullest. Obedience is the key to our success. Following his way—and not man's—will open up the door to many possibilities.

I am thankful for the desire to walk in the spirit. As I walk with the voice of God in my ear and do as He instructs me, I know that the treasure of wisdom—knowledge and understanding—is available to me.

Prayer
Dear Lord, Thank You for the opportunity to gain success through Your treasure of knowledge and understanding. Amen.

Word of the Day
Knowledge

Personal Meditations

Today's Prayer

75

Praise: My Shield and Protection

He grants good sense to the godly-his saints. He is their
shield, protecting them and guarding their pathways.
—Proverbs 2:7–8 (TLB)

Lady Wisdom asks, "Is God protecting you and guarding your pathway?"

In this season of our lives, there is a great need to pay attention to what God is telling us. It requires that we are keeping a sound mind and self-restraint and we are alert to what God is doing on the earth. All of this is possible by the practice of prayer and biblical meditation. We must arm ourselves with the knowledge and wisdom of God. With this insight, we are able to purposely follow the pathway of God, avoiding pitfalls and traps of the enemy.

The good sense that God grants us empowers us to move forward with confidence, knowing that God is our shield and protector. He is already scouting out the pathway and providing a clear road to travel. Our life will not be free from suffering; however, we will have the strength to resist the devil, and he will have to flee. As we surrender our will to God and are finished with intentional sins by pleasing ourselves and the world, we cannot spend our time thinking about ourselves, but we begin to think about what makes God happy. Having the mind of Christ fills us with joy and thanksgiving knowing that God is for us.

To utilize the good sense that God has given us will help us to avoid the unnecessary attacks from the enemy. We will know how to resist and fight against the inner desires that only lead to death. As we strengthen our prayer and praise muscles, we can overcome and break through to greater blessings. Amen!

Prayer
Dear Lord, Thank You for good sense. Thank You for being our shield, protector, and guard. Amen.

Word of the Day
Protection

Personal Meditations

Today's Prayer

76

Praise: Finding the Right Decision

He shows how to distinguish right from wrong,
how to find the right decision every time.
—Proverbs 2:9 (TLB)

Lady Wisdom asks, "Do you know how to find the right decision for the situation?"

Living by the spirit of wisdom has its advantages. We can distinguish between right and wrong. As we live in the spirit like God does, our spiritual eyes will become more open to God's will for our lives. We can see clearer; therefore we can make the right decisions every time.

It is necessary to develop a sound mind and use self-restraint with how we do things. We must consult the Holy Spirit first and let Him give us the information needed to be able to avoid the traps of the enemy. We can be alert and ready to defend what is right and just. We also need to be aware of others. Living a life of love helps to cover us from bitterness or envy. Love covers a multitude of wrongdoing and empowers us to love cordially and graciously without complaining.

As we exercise the gift of discernment, a divine endowment granted to us, we must employ it to find the right decision every time. It will benefit us as we use it by faith and are good stewards of wisdom and good sense. We are grateful to God for His extreme unmerited favor to us so we can know how to find the right decision every time. Amen.

Prayer
Dear Lord, Thank You for giving us divine favor so we can know how to find the right decision every time. Amen.

Word of the Day
Decision

Today's Prayer

77

Praise: Center of Your Being

For wisdom and truth will enter the very center
of your being, filling your life with joy.
—Proverbs 2:10 (TLB)

Lady Wisdom asks, "Are you praising God for increasing joy?"

When life becomes difficult, we can rest assured that God is in control of our lives. His wisdom and truth enters us and fills us with a knowing that God is for us! Therefore we do not need to jump to conclusions that God isn't present and looking out for us His eyes are watching our every move. What a great promise and word of encouragement for us to relax in God because He is looking out for us.

When we have imprinted the wisdom and truth of God in our hearts, then just when we need that insight, it will be revealed to us. There is glory in our presence, and His glory will be revealed in our situation. It is the glory in us that people see when we walk in the joy of the Lord. Embracing the message of wisdom opens up many doors and opportunities for us to give God glory and praise.

So if we allow wisdom and truth to be in the center of our hearts, then we can experience the joy. We can enjoy everyday life. We are doing what God says, and we are able to take what comes our way because we know that God knows what He is doing. He's got our best interests at heart.

Prayer
Dear Lord, Thank You for looking out for us. Help me to trust You because You know what You are doing. Amen.

Word of the Day
Center

78

Praise: Honor the Lord

Honor the Lord by giving him the first-part of all your
income and he will fill your barns with wheat and barley
and overflow your win vats with the finest wines,
—Proverbs 3:9–10 (TLB)

Lady Wisdom asks, "Are you honoring God with your income?"

I am thankful for the increase of all that God has to offer in my life.
There is a willingness to give and to give generously and graciously. The
spirit of generosity is first demonstrated with my willingness to honor
the Lord. Honoring the Creator and the one who gives me my identity
places me in a position to receive all He wants to fill me with. It is not
just financial blessings but also eternal blessings.

Each day I am becoming aware of the finite reality of this life. We are
so much more. We are eternal beings. God has given us the choice to
decide how we want to live. He says to us to choose this day whom we
want to serve: God or ourselves. I declare that I want to serve and love
God: Father, Son, and the Holy Ghost.

Loving God means I have to honor Him with my worldly possessions.
I have to love God with my body, mind/soul, and spirit. So therefore,
honoring the Lord puts me in the right place of humility and
reverence to God. What is so wonderful is that God is a giver
and He will not be outdone. He loves to fill and overflow us with
goodness. Amen.

Prayer

Dear Lord, Help me not to limit You and Your love for me with my limited way of thinking. I open my heart, mind/soul, and my body to be filled to the overflow with Your love so I can be generous and gracious like You. Thank You for all You have given me and all the blessings to come. Amen.

Word of the Day
Increase

Today's Prayer

79

Praise: What Wisdom Gives

Wisdom gives: A long, good life, Riches, Honor, Pleasure, and Peace.
—Proverbs 3:16–17 (TLB)

Lady Wisdom asks, "Are you grateful for what wisdom gives?"

I am grateful for what wisdom gives. Have the capacity to receive it and know that God has ordained us to have it all—riches, honor, pleasure, and peace. Yes, I am grateful. To gain all that God has assigned to us, we have to recognize that He is a rewarder of those who seek Him.

I confess that Jesus is my God, and I celebrate Him. I give God the praise for all of His miraculous wonders and His well-thought-out plans, which are secure and dependable. As we follow the God-given instructions, wisdom increases, and favor is granted. God cannot go against His Word. If He said it, He is obligated to bring the blessing to pass.

Our duties are to agree with His Word and seal it with praise and thanksgiving. Celebrating His goodness sets us up for more blessings as we honor His name. Therefore, let's sing the joys of His salvation and know that God's hand rests on our lives.

Prayer
Dear Lord, We thank You for being our unmovable rock. You are so good to us. We appreciate what wisdom gives us—a long life, riches, honor, pleasure, and peace. Amen.

Word of the Day
He Gives

Personal Meditations

Today's Prayer

80

Praise: Wisdom Tree of Life

Wisdom is a tree of life to those who eat her fruit;
happy is the man who keeps on eating it.
—Proverbs 3:18 (TLB)

Lady Wisdom asks, "Are you eating from the Wisdom Tree of Life?"

The Tree of Life has been defined as the symbol of a fresh start. When we eat the fruit of wisdom, we gain energy, good health, and a bright future. A tree grows old with wisdom, and as we mature in age, we can become wiser and smarter. Our decisions in life are based on applied knowledge of the ages. It has a track record of success.

Just like a tree, we are able to reproduce seeds from the fruit. This enables us to multiply in wisdom, knowledge, understanding, and insight. The result of eating this good fruit is that we are more confident and happier for it. I believe that the choices we make are more productive and dependable because they have been tested by experience.

Learning from the past gives us a measure of what does and does not work. We are more able to assess a situation and create a sustainable and successful solution. Success does make us happy. It also encourages us to keep on doing things that bring joy into our lives.

Prayer
Dear Lord, Thank You for giving us the tree of life so we can eat the fruit of success with joy. Amen.

Word of the Day
Wisdom Tree

Personal Meditations

Today's Prayer

Intensifying with the Tool of

THANKSGIVING

81

Thanksgiving: Do You Have a Song of Thanksgiving?

For as a man thinketh in his heart, so is he; Eat and
drink, saith he to thee; but his heart is not with thee.
—Proverbs 23:7 (KJV)

Lady Wisdom asks, "What are you singing? Are you singing for joy, or are you singing the blues?"

King David believed in the power of music. He set up a choir to sing in the tabernacle, day and night. He believed that God deserved to be praised untiringly; therefore he created the first tabernacle choir and gave them this song to sing. It was a song of thanksgiving to the Lord.

"Oh give thanks to the Lord and pray to him," they sang. "Tell the peoples of the world about his mighty doings. Sing to him yes sing his praises and tell of his marvelous works. Glory in his holy name. Let all rejoice who seek the Lord. Seek the Lord yes seek his strength. And seek his face untiringly" (1 Chronicles 16:8–11 TLB).

I believe that there is something about singing songs of praise and thanksgiving to God that just wakes up the soul and fills it with joy. The joy then gives us the strength to look at life from a more optimistic view. As we remember God's goodness to us, our hearts are transformed from feeling down and depressed to feeling alive and grateful.

There is a science of happiness that is being discovered for a more joyful life in our relationships, spirits, minds, and bodies. More and more people are realizing that what we meditate on can determine our mental and physical health. Singing allows us to bounce back from feelings of anxiety and defeat. An upbeat song can make us dance. Our body becomes more relaxed as we release the stress of the day. We become present in the moment and are able to feel the emotion of happiness, which can lead to lasting joy. It is important to infuse our days with more joy and fun. We can do this by getting up each morning and declaring, "This is the day that the Lord has made. We will rejoice and be glad in it."

Prayer
Dear Lord, Help me to release a song of thankfulness to You every day. I want to sing to You and tell others about how good You are. Amen.

Word of the Day
A Song

Personal Meditations

Today's Prayer

82

Thanksgiving: Recognizing the King

In everything you do put God first and he will direct
you and crown your efforts with success.
—Proverbs 3:6 (TLB)

Lady Wisdom asks, "Who are you recognizing as your king?"

People want a superhero, someone they can follow or look up to. In today's world with the increase of accessibility to so many people through the internet, it is possible to build a community around a leader or charismatic person. The big screen is able to paint a picture of what a person is looking for. The algorithms and search engines can discern what your habits and interests are. The Google search gives suggestions based on your history of what you are looking for in the search engine.

There is this longing to worship something. God placed this desire in our hearts. The question is, "Who will be the king of your life?" Zechariah 14:9 (AMPC) states, "And the Lord shall be King over all the earth; in that day the Lord shall be one [in the recognition and worship of men] and His name one." In other words, King Jesus will be the only God over all of the earth. Jesus is going to take His stand, and every knee is going to bow to Him.

I believe that this is the time to get to know who Jesus is. Discover Him for yourself. The first thing that can be done is to discover Him in scripture. Read through the gospels of Matthew, Mark, Luke, and John. Ask the Holy Spirit to reveal who Jesus is to you. Make it a personal discovery of what Jesus likes and dislikes and look at His interests and focus. Then pray to Jesus and seek Him out, and His kingdom agenda will allow us to obtain a personal relationship with the King of Kings.

Prayer

Dear Lord, I want to put You first in everything I do. Can you reveal to me who You are? Thank You in advance for all of the things You have done for me. Thank You for saving me. Amen.

Word of the Day
Everything

83

Thanksgiving: A Time to Be with Jesus

Be with wise men and become wise. Be with evil men and become
evil. Curses chase sinners, while blessings chase the righteous!
—Proverbs 13:20–21 (TLB)

Lady Wisdom asks, "Have you been spending time with wise words?"

Having an overloaded lifestyle robs us of the time we need to build and
sustain our relationship with King Jesus. We are overwhelmed with all
of the responsibilities and stresses of our daily life that we overlook what
is most important, time spent with Jesus. We end up pushing out the
most meaningful person in our life for a temporary fix. Other things
become a replacement for what matters the most.

Who knows what tomorrow holds? We must take the time to pay
attention to who and what matters the most. Putting God low on our
priority list sets us up for failure in every area of our lives. We must find
ourselves in the company of the Spirit so we can find out the essence of
who we are and what is most important.

Have you been feeling irritable and finding that something is robbing
you of your time and creativity? Does joy seem to allude you? Has life
become more about doing than being? These are the questions to ask
that may assist us in changing our mind-set from a mundane existence
to a joyful experience.

Here are some things to consider. Thinking about time and what it
means to lose it on things that are unimportant and not urgent will help
to redirect us to what is most important. Spending time recognizing
Jesus and His goodness to us can also be a great exercise in focusing on

having a thankful heart. Meditating on what God has revealed to us in our quiet times will again inspire us to be thankful. We will find that our spiritual cup will be overflowing with joy.

Prayer
Dear Lord, Help me to remember to take the time to give thanks and put You first in my day. Help me to choose You over other things by spending time in Your presence each day. Amen.

Word of the Day
Remember

Personal Meditations

Today's Prayer

84

Thanksgiving: My Everyday Life Is an Offering!

Honor the Lord by giving Him the first part of your
income, and he will fill your barns with wheat and barley
and overflow your wine vats with the finest wines.
—Proverbs 3:9 (TLB)

Lady Wisdom asks, "What is your spending telling you?"

As I was reading Romans 12:1–2 (MSG), I realized that my life is an offering to God. I am not giving myself to God in terms of what I want to give, but rather giving the best gift that God wants from me, which is a heart of thanksgiving. My sleeping, eating, going to work, and walking around life are an offering.

With an attitude that embraces what God has done for me with a heart of gratitude, God wants our acknowledgment of His love and goodness toward us. He wants us to say "thank you." We do not want to have an entitlement attitude that God has to do this for us or that our expectations are so ritualistic that we take God for granted.

By fixing our attention on God, we can be changed from the inside out. We can develop a knowing of what God likes and dislikes. We will be able to understand what He wants from us and be able to respond to His calling. We will find that our lives will have more meaning and purpose with a level of satisfaction. God will be bringing the best out of us in a creative and refreshing way. Seeing the world through His eyes gives us clear vision into our future. Maturing into what God would have us be opens up a level of responsibility, which leads to growth.

What we can do to give ourselves to God as an offering is to first reverence Him by spending time acknowledging His goodness. Having an eye for all that is good and perfect in the world, we can use this to stay in the place of thanksgiving, which will allow our view of others to change. Our cups become full with joy and will overflow. We can shift our ways to a more proverbs lifestyle of building and harvesting God's goodness.

Prayer
Dear Lord, I give my life to You as a daily offering of thanksgiving. Help me to see goodness and mercy in people and situations that I encounter during the day. Amen.

Word of the Day
Offering

Today's Prayer

85

Thanksgiving: Thank You for Provision

The good influence of godly citizens causes a city to prosper,
but the moral decay of the wicked drives it downhill.
—Proverbs 11:11 (TLB)

Lady Wisdom asks, "Are you building up your world with goodness or tearing it down?"

God provides for us through our work. His provision is so great that there is a surplus and plenty to go around. We are encouraged to pray and give thanks for our place of employment, community, and nation. Our prayers of gratitude can open up the doors to greater opportunity and prosperity. Seeking the peace and welfare of our place of residence brings the spirit of peace and blessings to the region.

What we do with our provision matters. It can hinder the flow of the blessing of prosperity. Do we eat the seed, or do we reinvest it to increase and grow? Our attitude of gratitude affects our actions. Are we going to hoard it, or are we going to give liberally to improving others?

Holding is a term used in bitcoin. It is when people do not sell or buy with the bitcoin. They just keep it and wait. What this does is limit the flow of activity and create a lack, making the value of bitcoin decrease. However, when there is a big dump of activity, the value of bitcoin increases because people want it.

It is the same for anything. When we hold our thanksgiving and praise, we are killing our relationship with others and God. Giving thanks and showing appreciation for others opens up the floodgates of blessing. Our generosity inspires others to give, starting a movement. God wants us to pray for and give thanks because it is the key to our blessings. By blessing others, we are blessed too. Blessing others with what we have increases our ability to be like God. God is a giver and provider, and He is a resource to our body, mind, and spirit.

Prayer
Dear Lord, Help me to give thanks for others and my provisions. Thank You for my workplace, community, and nation. Bless it all. Amen.

Word of the Day
Provision

Personal Meditations

Today's Prayer

86

Thanksgiving: Giving Thanks for Our Leaders

These are the proverbs of King Solomon of Israel, David's son; He wrote them to teach his people how to live- how to act in every circumstance, for he wanted them to be understanding, just and fair in everything they did.
—Proverbs 1:1–3 (TLB)

Lady Wisdom asks, "Who is leading you?"

Having godly leaders is a blessing! Leaders who are blessed with wisdom to make good decisions improve every institution in society. Having success works well for everyone, especially if the environment is supportive and creative. God's peace in the hearts of the people who lead sets the tone for a productive and safe environment. The feelings of peace and joy move throughout the workplace and spill over into every facet of life. Praying and blessing all people in positions of authority opens the door to godly change. They have the power and influence to fulfill God's purposes. Any time a king or ruler was willing to go God's way, the people benefited, and the country thrived.

One of the things we need to be mindful of is the words that come out of our mouths. It is easy to curse the leaders in positions, especially if they are not supportive and are very difficult to work for. It is important to let God do the judging and correcting. Praying for them and asking God to increase the positive things about them will set the atmosphere for change. Instead of cursing them, you will be blessing them. Thanking God in prayer for your boss will help you to monitor what you say about them.

We can lead a thankful, peaceable life with godliness and dignity if we allow God's presence into the workplace with praise and thanksgiving leading the way. With a thankful heart, we are able to address the difficult boss or leader with honor and respect. Honoring those who are in authority over us positions us for blessings.

Prayer
Dear Lord, Bless the leaders who are over me. Give them success in their activities and assignments. Grant us a peaceful workplace, community, and nation. Amen.

Word of the Day
Leadership

87

Thanksgiving: Different Perspectives Improve Our Lives

She who loves wisdom loves her own best
interest and will be a success.
—Proverbs 19:8 (TLB)

The intelligent man is always open to new ideas. In fact he looks for them.

—Proverbs 18:15 (TLB)

Lady Wisdom asks, "Are you listening to the viewpoint of wisdom?"

Being thankful for people who think differently from us opens up the way to new innovations and blessings. We were created to live in communities. Learning to appreciate our differences and work on our weaknesses and negative attitudes can bring harmony to any environment. Conflict is the number-one way of shutting down creativity. People begin to look out for their own best interests, disregarding the other person's needs. It becomes a very selfish environment, and people begin to hoard their resources.

The Bible tells us in everything—and that includes the workplace—to give thanks. By letting our supplications of thanksgiving go out to God in prayer, we are changing our focus from that of lack to blessing. We are able to bless the different perspectives and viewpoints as we look for the good, honorable, and worthy part. Philippians 4:6–8 tells us to whatever is true, just, pleasing, commendable, excellent, and worthy of praise, think on these things. Focusing on the positive changes our hearts and brings a freshness to any relationship.

What we want to see is a renewal of our spheres of influence into places of peace and joy. We want people to feel welcomed and appreciated for what they can contribute to our community. Sparks of creativity and innovation can lead to great success and prosperity in which everyone will benefit. Thankfulness can influence and bring joy to many.

Prayer
Dear Lord, Bless the people who are in my family, community, and workplace. Help me to see the best in them. Thank You for the people who bring a new perspective into my life. I want to appreciate their contributions. Amen.

Word of the Day
Improvement

Personal Meditations

Today's Prayer

88

Thanksgiving: How to Displace Worry

Happy is the man who is so anxious to be with me
(Lady Wisdom) that he watches for me daily at my gates
or waits for me outside my home! For whoever finds
me finds life and wins approval from the Lord.
—Proverbs 8:34 (TLB)

Lady Wisdom asks, "Are you spending time with me in prayer and praise?"

Displace worry out of the center of your life with praise and thanksgiving. When we fret or worry, it leads to many other negative feelings, which produce actions that can be very destructive. The good thing is that God knows our concerns. He can bring a sense of wholeness to everything we are experiencing. Everything can come together for good. The Holy Spirit will settle us down so we can think about increase and blessing.

It is a wonderful thing when Jesus takes away our worry from the center of our lives. He becomes the center of our joy. We all do best by filling our minds and thoughts with good things. Our meditations affect our outcomes. So meditating on things that are true, noble, reputable, authentic, and gracious instead of ugly and mean, we set ourselves up for more blessings. The beautiful things that make us thankful change our perspective on the world.

What we have to do is put this game-changer into practice. Be thankful! We have to realize that what we meditate on determines how we are going to act. Are we going to work peaceably with others, or are we going to worry? We have the choice, and we can decide to choose the excellent way—to be in harmony with others and God.

Prayer

Dear Lord, Help me to trust You and not to worry. I want to see the good in others and rejoice in what You have to produce in me, peace. Amen.

Word of the Day
Produce

89

Thanksgiving: There Is Power in Being Thankful!

If you exalt wisdom, she will exalt you. Hold her fast and she will lead
you to great honor; she will place a beautiful crown upon your head.
—Proverbs 4:8–9 (TLB)

Lady Wisdom asks, "Who are you applauding and lifting up?"

Our spirits and minds can be attuned to God's purpose and plan.
If we desire to walk in Him with diligence and fidelity, then we can
experience His heart. He is willing to give us an ear to hear what He
wants us to do. He has made it possible for us to acquire knowledge
and understanding of the ways that God works through His Word. As
we learn more of how He works, we will find ourselves moving and
doing like Him. We will know what to do and what not to do as we
please Him.

We need the strength to be focused and persistent. Moving in the joy of
the Lord, which is our strength, we can move forward with confidence.
Being thankful helps us to see what God is doing, and it helps to keep
our minds focused on the goodness of God. Biblical meditation fills
our mind with an optimistic attitude, which translates into gratitude
and praise.

Giving thanks to God daily positively changes our mind-set. Pausing
to acknowledge God's attentive presence in our lives makes us want to
move into singing and rejoicing. It sparks a heart filled with love for our
Savior Jesus. There is power in being thankful.

Prayer
Dear Lord, Help me to remember that You are always actively present in my life to give me what I need to please You. Thank You for giving me a heart filled with gratitude and thanksgiving. Amen.

Word of the Day
Attuned

Deepening with the Tool of

WORSHIP

90

Worship: The Work of Worship

Carry out my instructions; don't forget them,
for they will lead you to real living.
—Proverbs 4:13TLB

Lady Wisdom asks, "What are the assignments and instructions given to you to do?"

The Levites were assigned to assist the priests in the work of worship in God's house. Whatever needed to be done to present the temple for worship came under the responsibilities of them. The Lord showed the priests how to delegate the work so they could be focused on ministering to Him. They were present for morning prayers, thanksgiving to God, and praising Him as they did their duties. They were present for all of the services and were on regular duty to serve God according to their assigned tasks. They worked alongside the priests as their companions in the ministry of holy worship.

Preparations for worship are important to the quality of our ability to hear from God. When we take the time to sing songs of praise, to take communion, to pray, and to read the Bible, we are setting ourselves up to enter into the presence of God. King David wrote that we must enter into His gates with thanksgiving and into His courts with praise. We need to be thankful and bless His name.

Each of us has been assigned the work of worship. We are priests to our God. Just like how Aaron was assigned and ordained to work in the Holy of Holies, to serve God and bless His name, we too are assigned to serve and bless the Lord. We must take care of our worship in our hearts because that is where the Holy Spirit lives. We must be on regular duty to do the will of our Father God and fulfill His plan.

Prayer
Dear Lord, I want to be a reliable worker in Your kingdom. Help me to remember the work of worship and not to substitute it for busywork. Amen.

Word of the Day
Reliable

Personal Meditations

Today's Prayer

91

Worship: The Heart of Worship

Fear of man is a dangerous trap, but to trust in God means safety.
—Proverbs 29:25 (TLB)

Lady Wisdom asks, "Why not trust God and let your confidence rise?"

What is pushing you to your knees? It may just be what God is using to keep you in a position of worship. Things in life may get you down, but don't stay there. Worship! God tells us that His grace is enough and all we need. We depend on Him, and through our worship, He gets the glory. We are also rewarded for our diligence and dedication in worship. We are favored to have Christ's strength overtake our weakness. We can then say, "In all things give thanks!"

Let our worship become a portal to God's power. Our worship will make us strong as we humble ourselves in the presence of the Lord. When we humble ourselves before Him, He then lifts us up and fights for us. We just have to maintain an attitude of gratitude and praise as we adore His name. It becomes a love-fest.

How do we worship? In Spirit and in truth, we go before the Father in Jesus's name and the aid of the Holy Spirit. Jesus's blood gives us access to the throne room of grace. There we can find peace and rest for our souls. We can be comforted and made strong in the strength of the Lord. Our weakness gives us entrance into the Holy of Holies. Our confidence rises, and we become overcomers and victorious in Christ.

Prayer
Dear Lord, Help me to find that place of power in the heart of worship in Jesus's name. Amen.

Word of the Day
Heart

Today's Prayer

92

Worship: Working for the King Is My Worship!

Blessed is the man who reveres God, but the man
who doesn't care is headed for serious trouble.
—Proverbs 28:14 (TLB)

I, Wisdom, give good advice and common sense. Because of my strength,
kings reign in power. I show the judges who is right or wrong.

—Proverbs 8:14 (TLB)

Lady Wisdom asks, "Who do you respect: God or people?"

God has been called Creator and Founder of the world. He knows
just how things were designed and manufactured, and He wants us to
distribute His products of righteousness, peace, and joy to the world. To
worship God in spirit and in truth requires that we surrender our will
and plans to God. It is not a burden to do so because we are working
for the King of Kings and the Lord of Lords. He is a wonderful boss
who offers us great benefits and an inheritance. When we are focused on
Christ's agenda, then we are giving Him our reasonable service. We are
putting aside our agenda for His. The Word of God becomes fulfilled
in our lives because He opens to us the books that have been written
about us before we were born. The revelation of His plan comes to us in
our dreams. We respond to the calling, which is our worship.

I have a new song to sing to the Lord. This song comes from my heart-
melody and verse. God does not want me to be selfish with this song but
to share it with the world so everyone can say with me, "God is good,
and His mercy endures forever." I desire to tell everyone each day how

awesome my Jesus is. This is the good news. I want to take his message of love, peace, and hope to the nations.

One way that we can worship the king in our work is to do and serve others with joy. Our attitude determines our happiness level. Moving away from what is best for me is a process of growing in grace. The process speeds up when I worship God by practicing His presence in the spirit of worship as I serve Him and others.

Prayer
Dear Lord, I know You are the wise, wonderful, and brilliant God. I want to tell others of Your awe-inspiring, majestic ways. Help me to radiate Your beauty and shine for You. Amen.

Word of the Day
Working

93

Worship: Be Intentional in Your Worship!

Happy is the man who is so anxious to be with me that he watches
for me daily at my gates or waits for me outside my home! For
whoever finds me finds life and wins approval from the Lord.
—Proverbs 8:34–35 (TLB)

Lady Wisdom asks, "Are you being intentional in your worship?"

God is telling us to stay wide awake in prayer. We can do this when we
are intentional in our daily devotion to God. The Bible encourages us
to get up early in the morning and seek the Lord's will. When we take
the time to ask Him for wisdom for the day, we will find that things
will go smoother. Life becomes a worshipful experience.

Being intentional in our worship allows us to direct our attention to
God's will. We are able to remove other distractions and give the Holy
Spirit the opportunity to speak into our lives. When we do not give
Him any time, we limit our ability to flourish, and our productivity
level diminishes. Taking time to discover God's will for the day is the
best way to worship. It sets us up for great things ahead.

God's glory will be just around the corner because the Holy Spirit is
instructing us. Lady Wisdom speaks into our lives and gives us the
opportunity to move into the promises that God has for us. We can
accomplish this intentional lifestyle by having morning devotion and
prayer. Finding a quiet place in our house and also then stilling our
mind with praise and biblical meditation, we are able to worship God
in spirit and in truth.

Prayer
Dear Lord, Help me to be intentional about my worship to You. I want to hear what You have to say to me so my life can give You all of the glory. Amen.

Word of the Day
Intentional

Personal Meditations

Today's Prayer

94

Worship: Cultivate Love through Worship

When she speaks, her words are wise, and kindness
is the rule for everything she says.
—Proverbs 31:26 (TLB)

Lady Wisdom asks, "Are you cultivating love and worship?"

Demonstrating love for others is the ultimate worship expression to God. God is love, and when we are loving to others, we are being like Him. He is pleased with our worship and comes and joins us with many blessings. The benefit of worshiping God with a spirit of love is that we become healed too.

The issues of life that seem to plague us are resolved in the Lord's presence. Here, there is peace and joy, and we are made righteous through His love, which was demonstrated on the cross. We can cultivate an inner beauty that all can see. Our life becomes a testimony of what we can do when we are surrendered to His way of being and doing things.

We want people to be captivated by our inner beauty and lifestyle of wisdom. Cultivating inner beauty requires that we spend time worshipping God. He will beautify us by showing us what needs to be changed, what we need to do differently, and how to do it. We will become more gentle, gracious, and kind taking on the characteristics of the Holy Spirit, who will teach us the ways of God.

Prayer
Dear Lord, I want to be a woman of substance who loves God, who therefore can love others too. Help me to cultivate the inner beauty of a gentle and kind spirit. I want to move and be filled with the spirit of love, joy, and peace. Teach me Your ways. Amen.

Word of the Day
Great Substance

Personal Meditations

Today's Prayer

95

Worship: Be a Blessing!

She sews for the poor, and generously gives to the needy.
—Proverbs 31:19–20 (TLB)

Lady Wisdom asks, "How are you blessing others?"

One way that we can actively worship God is by being a blessing. How we speak to others is a wonderful testimony of how God is blessings our lives. It is our reasonable service to make sure that our lives are lining up with our words. Cultivating inner beauty makes it easy to be gentle, gracious, and kind toward others. God delights in our acts of kindness. He sees it as if we are desiring to be like Him.

When you are doing things to help others, you are doing well. You cannot be stopped because God will look at your efforts and steps of faith. He will provide the necessary help and encouragement so you can continue to be a blessing. As you go about doing good, others will become interested in joining your movement.

We have to see that good deeds fill our day. It really does not cost us anything to do these things. Say kind words toward others. Be helpful. Keep the peace and help others to find peaceful ways of doing things. Also listen and respond to needs and concerns with kindness. Smile!

Prayer
Dear Lord, I want to be a blessing to others. Show me how I can give and be like You, spending love, joy, and peace. Amen.

Word of the Day
Blessing

Personal Meditations

Today's Prayer

96

Worship: God's Word Will Always Prosper

A wise man's words express deep streams of thought.
—Proverbs 18:4 (TLB)

Lady Wisdom asks, "Are you thinking the way God thinks, and are you working the way God works?"

Isaiah 55:8, 11 (KJV) states, "For my thoughts are not your thoughts, neither are your ways my ways, saith the Lord ... So shall my word be that goeth forth out of my mouth: it shall not return unto me void, but it shall accomplish that which I please, and it shall prosper in the thing whereto I sent it."

We can live with the assurance that God's Word will always prosper. God has a way of making things work out for our good. What is required from us is the willingness to return to Him and ask Him to forgive us. Then we have to get back on track and do what He has instructed us to do. God is patient. His patience is demonstrated by giving us the time we need to mature in Him.

Clearly the Lord does not think like how we do. He is very much aware of our limited understanding. He works in a different way. Time spent with the Holy Spirit gives us the opportunity to learn the ways of wisdom. His wisdom surpasses the way we work. He is the creator of the universe; therefore His thinking is beyond our earthbound knowledge. There are so many mysteries that science is still trying to figure out. As soon as the researchers discover something new, it becomes old and outdated. Some new discovery is made and continues to build on what little knowledge mankind thinks he knows.

One thing is true: God's Word is powerful and cannot come back empty-handed. Isaiah 55 (Message Bible) states, "So will the words that come out of my mouth not come back empty-handed. They'll do the work I sent them to do, they'll complete the assignment I gave them."

Therefore, it is important that we seek God every day. Praying to Him and worshipping His goodness, abandoning our thinking, will make room for Lady Wisdom to give us fresh insight and understanding of the ways of our Creator God.

Prayer
Dear Lord, I desire to seek Your will. I am alive by praying to you. Help me to abandon my ways of being and doing things. I want to think like You and work the way you do. I am thankful that Your Word will grow in me and produce seed and food for our hungry soul. I want to accomplish my assignment with joy. Amen.

Word of the Day
Thoughts

Personal Meditations

Today's Prayer

97

Worship: Entering into My Promised Land Is My Act of Worship!

For whoever finds me finds life and wins approval from the Lord.
—Proverbs 8:35 (TLB)

Lady Wisdom asks, "Are you entering into your Promised Land?"

When we walk by faith and not by sight, we are demonstrating worship to our God. We are actually saying, "Lord, I trust you!" This movement of obedience activates a release of courage and strength. God backs what we are doing because He wants to see His Word performed and brought into manifestation on the earth. He is a God of results. His Word must accomplish what He has determined for it to do.

It is so easy to be caught up in our own limitations that we forget who is making things happen for us. It is God Himself, the Creator of the universe, who has invested in us. He expects a return on His investments. Therefore, we can put aside our own fears and lean into what He is saying so we can get the instructions right and follow them to the T.

When God speaks to us and calls us out of a comfortable place, it is because He has something greater in store for us to do and to have. He has a "Promised Land" designed to bring out the best in us. He said to Abram in the Bible, "Go from your country and your kindred and your father's house to the land that I will show you. I will make of you a great nation and I will bless you and make your name great so that you will be a blessing. I will bless those who bless you and the one who curses you I will curse; and in you all the families of the earth shall be blessed" (Genesis 12:1–3). This promise made to Abram is also made to us. God has something great that He wants us to do. However, are we ready to listen and obey the voice of the Lord?

What we want the most—what is lacking in our lives—God wants to give it to us. Sometimes we are not even aware of the thing because we have buried it in our subconscious mind. But when God calls us out, He knows what we want and desire, and He is going to speak to that desire that He placed in us.

Abram and Sarah wanted to have a child, an heir to his wealth. God came to him with this proposition that He would give them a two-part blessing of land and children. Abram and Sarah could not resist because that was what they wanted in their heart. They had all they needed. They were wealthy according to worldly standards. However, God knew what they were lacking and wanted to fulfill that desire, which He placed in them.

God has promises that He has decided to make to us. The question is: Are we willing to be honest with ourselves and realize that there is more to life than what we are experiencing right now? God wants us to trust Him, just like how Abraham and Sarah trusted Him by stepping out in faith and leaving our comfort zone. So let's get moving and step out and see what great thing God has for us in this new coming season of 2020.

Prayer
Dear Lord, I know You have a great promise for me and a dream that is larger than my mind can comprehend. Please give me the capacity to embrace what you have ordained for me and start walking by faith to my Promised Land. Amen.

Word of the Day
Promise

Today's Prayer

98

Worship: God's Masterpiece

And how happy I was with what he created—his
wide world and all his family of mankind!
—Proverbs 8:31 (TLB)

Lady Wisdom asks, "Have you consulted the Creator about your life?"

The Bible states, "For we are God's masterpiece. He has created us anew in Christ Jesus, so we can do the good things he planned for us long ago" (Ephesians 2:10 NLT). If this is the case, then we need to know what God had in mind when He created us. I am curious to know what the good things that he planned for me are. I think I would be able to avoid a lot of wasted time trying to figure out who I am and what I am about. I can ask Him.

Thankfully, God does not want me guessing about my purpose and His plans. I think that if we ask Him and listen, then we will know. Sometimes however, we do not want to go the way of God. We have our own ideas of what we want to do, or worse, we let society dictate what we are to be and do. We leave it up to our short view of the world and life. Thankfully we can move past that and learn what God has to say in the matter. It is never too late to discover the true you. We can live and love well, discovering who God says we are. That's good news!

So the question is: How do we go about finding out God's plan for our lives? The quick answer is to ask Him. He has created us anew in Jesus because He wants us to advance the kingdom of God here on earth. He has the master plan, the blueprint. Through biblical meditation in which we ponder, personalize, practice, praise, and pray, we will learn and gain wisdom, understanding, and insight to what God wants us to do. It is also a daily walk with God. It has a lot of benefits, but also it has a suffering and testing too. One thing I know for sure: if God is for you, who can be against you? With the aid of the Holy Spirit, the teacher, we will be beautifully built to give God glory. Amen.

Prayer
Dear Lord, I worship You and thank You for making me Your unique, one-of-a-kind masterpiece for Your honor and glory. Help me to trust You enough to let You do the work in me. Amen.

Word of the Day
Masterpiece

Personal Meditations

Today's Prayer

99

Worship: Acknowledge the Lord by Your Worship

Trust in the Lord with all thine heart; and lean
not unto thine own understanding. In all thy ways
acknowledge him, and he shall direct thy paths.
—Proverbs 3:5–6 (KJV)

Lady Wisdom asks, "Who has your heart?"

Every day we trust in things and believe they will perform for us, just as we expect them to. We do not doubt what will happen because of our level of faith. Our past history with the object has been consistently good so we are willing to relax and believe in the object's integrity. For example, we sit in our favorite chair, and we believe it will hold us up because of its consistent performance. We deem it reliable. Trusting the chair's ability to hold us up is not an issue. We just know that it is.

When we are able to trust in the Lord, then we are willing to not rely on our own opinions. Before we do anything, God would have to be consulted. Relying on Him to guide us will become second nature. The Lord is willing to lead and guide us through life. Do we know Him intimately? Do we trust His words? The deciding factor will be determined if we have cultivated a good, godly history with the Creator.

Proverbs 3 tells us to first trust in the Lord. It is a decision that we have to want to make. Will we have faith? If we are convinced that the Lord can be trusted, then are we ready to move into the next level of commitment to Him and His Word? Second, do not rely on your own opinions. There is a time when we have to give up trying to estimate the outcome of the issue. Instead take on a new understanding of who God is and an appreciation for what He can do. We are convinced that His Word is dependable. Third, this confidence is acquired by a change of our heart. Whose Word are we going to believe? Fourth, there must be a release of our lives to Him in confidence, letting Him lead the way. He becomes the chief decision-maker. We follow His instructions. Fifth, as we develop an intimate understanding and reliance of who He is and what He requires us to do, we can move forward. We are confident of our success, and we relax in the reliability of His words.

Prayer
Dear Lord, I worship You with my obedience to Your Word. I know that Your words are trustworthy. I can count on Your faithfulness to me. Thank You for loving me and giving me a bright, exciting, and successful future. Amen.

Word of the Day
Acknowledge

Personal Meditations

Today's Prayer

100

Worship: Here Is My Worship!

Charm can be deceptive and beauty doesn't last, but a woman who fears and reverences God shall be greatly praised. Praise her for the many fine things she does. These good deeds of hers shall bring her honor and recognition from the leaders of the nations.
—Proverbs 31:30–31 (TLB)

Lady Wisdom asks, "Is the pace and load of your life stealing your praise and worship for God?"

Reverencing God takes time. Are you wasting your time, or are you using it to receive vital information for your day? When we respect God, it is easy to give Him the best time of our day. There is an eternal value within our limited time on the Planet Earth. Time cannot be reclaimed; therefore we must utilize it wisely.

We have a choice to make. Do we live an overloaded lifestyle, or do we live a proverbs lifestyle filled with meaning and wisdom? Some signs of living a lifestyle that is not productive or honoring God are: having a sense of being overwhelmed by people and things, feeling that things are stealing your creativity and joy, working too hard, or doing things rather than being fulfilled in your purpose.

There are things that we can do to get into the flow of God, moving to His beat. Be intentional. Trust God's plan for your life. Align your actions with God's plan. Take actions that reflect a positive vision of a God-directed future. With prayer and biblical meditation, we can make sound choices that are wise and meaningful and will leave a positive impact on others. The results will be an exciting life, healed relationships, positive legacies, and an eternal impact on the world.

Prayer

Dear Lord, Thank You for giving me a desire to be wise. I am grateful for the plans You have for me. Help me to listen well and then to obey them. I know Your intentions are to bless me. Give me the patience to learn Your ways and walk in the confidence of Your love. Amen.

Word of the Day
Reverence

Today's Prayer

101

Worship: Private Walk with Jesus

Charm can be deceptive and beauty doesn't last, but a woman who fears and reverences God shall be greatly praised.
—Proverbs 31:30 (TLB)

Lady Wisdom asks, "Are you ready to walk with God?"

Each of us is given an opportunity to have a private, individual walk with Jesus. A relationship that can and will change your life forever begins with asking Jesus to come into our lives and be the Lord of our lives. His kingship over our decisions sets us up for greater things. The Son of God now employs us. We get our assignments and instructions from Him through the Holy Spirit, the teacher and guide.

Time spent with Jesus is time well spent. Our engaging Him daily no matter what comes our way empowers us to be victorious in every situation. He has the inside scoop about everything. The good thing is that He has given us the Holy Spirit to teach us the details and to be inside of us so that there is no limit to advice and guidance that we can receive. We can have moment-by-moment revelation on how to deal with situations. We can walk in the confidence of the Word of God because we have written instructions in the Bible. Lady Wisdom speaks to us!

It is our responsibility to continue to grow in strength with the knowledge and understanding of God's truth in our hearts. We can be assured that it is God who has taught us all these things because we can look to His Word through biblical meditation and time spent in His presence. The words found in Proverbs provide the wisdom to experience a godly lifestyle pleasing to God. We are empowered to prosper. We have the blueprint, and it guides us in the right direction for success. We will become fully mature and perfectly prepared to fulfill any assignment God gives us.

Prayer

Dear Lord, Thank You for the opportunity to have a personal relationship with You. I want to advance, strengthened as I grow in the truth of Your Word. I want a heart that is wrapped up in Your will and purpose for my life. Thank You for teaching me Your Word by the guidance of Holy Spirit. Help me to do my part by listening and obeying You. Amen.

Word of the Day
Personal Relationship

Personal Meditations

Today's Prayer

Printed in the United States
By Bookmasters